# Million Dollar

## Dollar
### Selling
### Techniques

**Other Books in The Million Dollar Round Table Series**

*Million Dollar Prospecting Techniques*
*Million Dollar Closing Techniques*

# Million Dollar

# Dollar

# Selling

# Techniques

THE MILLION DOLLAR ROUND TABLE
CENTER FOR PRODUCTIVITY

JOHN WILEY & SONS, INC.

New York • Chichester • Weinheim • Brisbane • Singapore • Toronto

Copyright © 1999 by The MDRT Center for Productivity. All rights reserved.

Published by John Wiley & Sons, Inc.

Published simultaneously in Canada.

This publication is designed to provide accurate and authoritative information in regard to the subject matter covered. It is sold with the understanding that the publisher is not engaged in rendering professional services. If professional advice or other expert assistance is required, the services of a competent professional person should be sought.

Designations used by companies to distinguish their products are often claimed as trademarks. In all instances where the author or publisher is aware of a claim, the product names appear in Initial Capital letters. Readers, however, should contact the appropriate companies for more complete information regarding trademarks and registration.

*Library of Congress Cataloging-in-Publication Data:*

Million dollar selling techniques / The Million Dollar Round Table
   Center for Productivity.
      p.    cm.
   Includes index.
   ISBN 0-471-32549-X (pa. : alk. paper)
    1. Selling.  2. Selling—Insurance, Life.  I. The Million Dollar
Round Table (Park Ridge, Ill.).  Center for Productivity.
HF5438.25.M5692    1999
368.32'0068'8—dc21                    99-25932

10  9  8  7  6  5  4  3  2  1

# CONTENTS

## Chapter 3

## Chapter 4

# INTRODUCTION

Selling is universally accepted as one of the most important ingredients in the success or failure of most business ventures. Whether goods or services are being sold, the transaction from seller to buyer is a bridge that has to be constructed by skilled professionals who know their craft.

The premise of this book is that you have already decided on sales as a career, and now it's time to raise the bar. Why the title *Million Dollar Selling Techniques*? Because the core information you are about to receive is directly culled from one of the world's most prestigious sales organizations—The Million Dollar Round Table. Before getting to the details of selling, let's address most readers' question: "What is The Million Dollar Round Table?"

In 1927, thirty-two sales professionals gathered together in Memphis, Tennessee, to share sales ideas. They expected that the synergy of the group would enhance the professional skills of each participant. These sales professionals sold life insurance. Today, the objectives of that group have grown into an international organization of nearly 19,000 members in 40 countries, and have expanded throughout the financial services spectrum.

The Million Dollar Round Table commands universal respect. From a humble beginning, it has grown into the premier sales organization in the world. What is the MDRT magic? Over a long period of time, it has developed a set of core values that bind this prestigious organization together. These values nourish and sustain it, and they have made it the great organization that it is today. What better way to introduce this book and what the MDRT is all about than to articulate a number of these values and suggest how they can help you realize your full professional and human potential.

MDRT's most important value is *productivity,* on both a professional and a human level. The Round Table was founded on a level of production that set the highest standard. Today, it represents the top six percent of sales representatives in the world. Within the organization, however, there are two additional levels of productivity: at three times and at six times the basic entry requirements. As a prestigious sales organization, its philosophy is to "dream big dreams" and turn those dreams into reality.

In 1962, Dr. Mortimer Adler introduced an emphasis on human productivity to MDRT. Dr. Adler challenged MDRT members to understand the intrinsic need of all human beings—particularly, successful human beings—to reach both inside and outside themselves so that more meaningful lives can be achieved.

The ideas Dr. Adler presented came at a perfect time. The members of The Million Dollar Round Table had reached a point where they realized that sales success was not enough; that life is more than the sum total of what a person does for a living; that who an individual is must be regarded as more important than what an individual does. Dr. Adler suggested that some aspects of life allow a person to simply live, and other aspects permit a person to live well. The Round Table adopted what it now calls "the Whole Person Concept," described as a balance of seven vital life parts: (1) health, (2) family, (3) spiritual, (4) education, (5) financial, (6) service, and (7) career. By definition, whole persons are engaged in a lifetime quest to achieve balance and congruity in all aspects of their lives, and they continually seek to develop their full human potential.

The late Grant Taggart, an MDRT Past President, expressed the Whole Person Concept this way: "Personally, I believe in the acquisition of property and the making of money, but I contend such is not the all-important thing. Someone has said that when you sum it all up success isn't gold, it isn't in doing some deed that is bold. For the money we make or the houses we build mean nothing the moment one's voice has been stilled. But he or she has succeeded who, when he or she has gone, in the hearts of people is still living on." This philosophy has made MDRT sales professionals the successes they are today.

MDRT's *sharing and caring spirit* is a value that is cherished by its entire membership. Born at the original meeting in 1927, it has become a hallmark of the organization. MDRT has developed a rich tradition of sharing knowledge for the benefit of its members, its clients, and its members' companies. An unselfish concern for each other reflects a truly unique and positive quality.

MDRT's *commitment to excellence* is another value that pervades the organization. Nowhere is this value more evident than at the Annual Meeting, considered to be the finest sales meeting in the world. The greatest tribute paid to this meeting is that many MDRT members spend more than ten percent of their annual income to attend it. MDRT's commitment to excellence is validated by more than 1,200 members who actively serve the organization each year. MDRT's professional staff is a model for other sales organizations around the world. Superior performance has become MDRT's minimum standard.

In 1969, MDRT member Marshall Wolper challenged each of his MDRT associates: *"Always stay over your head."* His basic premise: Don't be afraid to try a new market because you have limited knowledge. One doesn't learn how to sail by reading a book. Jump in and give it your very best; you will learn by doing, and you will grow by working diligently in your new selling endeavors.

Dr. Alec McKenzie gave the organization another important value with his philosophy of *time management:* "No one has enough time, but everyone has all there is." Through McKenzie, MDRT associates learned about time wasters and the importance of delegating tasks to others. By practicing time management, sales professionals can spend their time doing the job they do best—meeting prospects and clients to uncover their problems and then solve them. MDRT sales professionals are, first and foremost, problem solvers.

A reinforced value for MDRT members is the importance of *goal setting.* Members need to know what they want from their business and personal lives and then set their goals accordingly. Goal setting enables sales professionals to have a track on which to run, and an ability to measure their progress. MDRT members have learned that one can achieve what one's mind can conceive. Dream "big dreams," and then set your goals to realize your dreams.

The Round Table has stressed the value of *professionalism,* defined as being a professional in all activities. MDRT sales professionals firmly believe that they must be good at who they are and what they do. Although many other values could be mentioned, the one that should be highlighted is that MDRT expects its members to take the high road and demonstrate, by their leadership, that it is not enough to do what is legal or even what is ethical. They must always choose to do what is right. They firmly believe that one is never contrite for doing the right thing, and taking the high road in all facets of life is the right thing to do.

What is the result of accepting the MDRT value system and the Whole Person Concept? Quite simply, phenomenal sales success—sales success that is transferred to you throughout the pages ahead.

# Chapter 1

# Selling Philosophy

A s a sales professional, your performance begins and ends with your philosophy on selling. Your ambitions, your attitude toward selling, and your conviction regarding what you sell all comprise your sales philosophy.

Without exception, the sales philosophies of MDRT members are solid and rank among the best in the world of sales. These sales professionals do not have to be told that this is a highly competitive world. The essence of their salesmanship is their ability to meet the competition.

What is the purpose of creating a favorable climate before selling begins? It helps guarantee that a sale is made by you for your products or services. Why expend effort to convince prospects that each argument they offer in resistance is a false one? So that a sale can be closed by you.

Some people may think that such selling has little to do with competition, but they are mistaken. In a sales situation, you are competing not only with other sales professionals who have the same or very similar products, but also with people who are selling entirely different products for a share of the dollars in your prospects' wallets. Whether they realize it or not, furniture sellers are in competition with the butcher shop and the restaurant and the movie house.

The best way for you to meet your competition is to pretend to ignore it—with an emphasis on the word "pretend." By showing prospects the qualities and advantages of your products or services, rather than deprecating what your competition is offering, you can make the competitive product suffer by comparison, without eroding your own integrity.

Nothing antagonizes a potential customer more than a frontal attack on the competition. It is in poor taste, it proves nothing about what you are trying to sell, and it is completely unnecessary. You can gain the same advantage by presenting the pluses of your offer rather than the drawbacks of the rival offer.

Sometimes, sales professionals sit back and dream of a selling world without competition. That scene is not merely an idle daydream; it is a frightening nightmare. Without competition, this would not be a desirable world in which to buy, sell, or live. The competitive spirit keeps quality up and prices down. Competition keeps sellers' wits sharp. There would be an extremely low level of selling, and hence a low standard of living, if there was no need to go out and meet the competition at all times. Yet how few are the people who know how to meet their competitors!

Let's meet the competition. First, as a sales professional, you must know and understand the competition, and face other sales professionals' products and offers in a realistic manner. You must never distort or close your mind to reality. The other sales professionals are good—but you are better. They sell fine products, but your products are superior.

Always feel that you are the best and without equal. Be aglow and afire with what you are selling. At the same time, don't sell your competition short. Understand that your competition is capable, but not as capable as you. Understand that their products are good, but never as excellent as yours.

And even if, within the private recesses of your mind, you are forced to admit that your competition's offer is a better one, you can always find superior features in your offer. Seize on those features and play them up; keep returning to them; believe in them with honesty and sincerity, and magnify them in the interviews until they become the central points in your sale.

From every standpoint, integrity is basic. Professionals selling any goods and services learn early in their careers that a reputation for undeviating honesty can open more doors and sell more business than any other single asset. Public opinion suggests that if a prospect were candidly addressing a sales professional, he or she would interpret integrity in some of these ways:

- ✓ "As a sales professional, I expect you to be strictly ethical in all of your dealings with me."

- ✓ "Keep your word. Show up when you say you will. Follow through on what you promise. When your sales talk opens with a request for five minutes of my time, I resent your carrying on for twenty minutes."

- ✓ "Point out product limitations. I must have the full story of just what this product will do and what it will not do. Don't let me dangle until after misfortune strikes and only then find out that the product doesn't work correctly."

- ✓ "Don't give me evasive answers to potentially embarrassing questions. I appreciate frankness."

- ✓ "If you tell me confidential information about somebody else, I am suspicious. It occurs to me that you will just as readily leak personal information about me."

- ✓ "Be loyal to your product and your organization. Don't break down the great confidence I have in what you sell."

- ✓ "Ask me to buy your product only when you sincerely believe that your recommendation is the best solution to my needs!"

One successful MDRT professional says this cornerstone is his base for sales integrity: "I try always to put myself in my prospects' shoes and recommend to them the kind of products that I would like to have recommended to me." Following this practice, he has always had a reliable standard of measurement— he sells products that are right for his clients.

Is such a standard of measure practical? It's not only practical—it's necessary. That's the conclusion reached, every day, by thousands of successful sales professionals whose sales strategy is soundly based on service in their public interest. Perhaps you are already thinking in terms of specifics.

Why not apply two simple tests to every sale you hope to make?

1. Am I reasonably certain my prospects have a definite need for the products I recommend?

2. Have I tried to help my prospects understand clearly all aspects of how my products will work, including their benefits and limitations?

Whatever you are selling, your prospects rely on your integrity to provide the right answers for them. The better you do your job, the better their opinions of you.

*Your sales philosophy must be rooted in motivation.*

Some people are born motivated, or so it seems. Others become motivated through experiences early in life. Through our different experiences, we change. With each experience, we adjust our goals in the common belief that if we are not motivated, we will not "make it big" or achieve our dreams.

Most MDRT sales professionals agree with that premise. They don't feel that things "just happen," or that, through meditation, predetermination, or providence alone, a person can achieve success. Becoming successful takes more than that. They believe in being in the right place at the right time, but working hard and having a passion for work are what create opportunities.

One key ingredient of motivation is the competitive spirit of an individual, and this can surface at any age. How many times have you heard that the person elected in high school as the "most likely to succeed" actually turned out to *be* the most successful? Until we learn to read people's minds, we will never be able to predict (with any high degree of accuracy) the consistent winners in advance.

For years, sales professionals have thought and philosophized about motivation. Many have reached the conclusion that for motivation to work most effectively, it must come from both internal and external sources.

Internal motivation has been described as the "burn"—the drive or the desire—to be your best, to reach your potential, to live the good life, and to serve others. Any successful sales professional has qualities that could be added to this list; but a person who has these qualities has an outstanding chance of becoming successful.

Nonetheless, internal sources alone will not sustain the drive that is needed to achieve maximum potential. External motivation is essential, and it starts with the five-year-old child looking up to his or her father or mother; the freshman looking up to the senior; the junior sales professional looking up to the consistent top-of-the-mountain sales superstar.

Maybe the external motivator is a former President of the United States, a sports or entertainment celebrity, a member of a religious order, or a mentor. Is there someone in your life for whom you have tremendous respect and admiration? It's not that you want to *be* that person; you just want to see yourself in the same light. This is not worship, it's admiration. Plain and simple, it's an intense respect for someone who has reached his or her dream, and who motivates you to reach yours. You must tell yourself, "If he or she can do it, so can I."

This external pull, added to the internal push, is a powerful combination. A person who possesses both stands an excellent chance of being able to meet or exceed his or her goals and dreams.

There are other forms of external motivation, too. Among them is *recognition.* The following scenario describes the importance of recognition. You are a 12-year-old and you're playing baseball. You're guarding third base, pounding your mitt, going through the motions, playing as well as you can, maintaining a positive attitude. You look into the stands. Your parents aren't in their seats. They must be late. You continue to play, you're intense, you want to do well, you can't wait to get up to bat. In the fourth inning, you look into the stands again. Your parents are sitting there, and it's impossible to describe the transformation that takes place within you. Now it's a new ballgame, a new ground ball, a new time at bat. Now it really counts because your parents are watching. Your face flushes, your skin is tingling. "Please, God, please, let me glove the grounders and get a base-hit later, please."

At age thirty, fifty, or seventy, you won't be pounding your mitt through the leather; but you should be able to remember how it felt. In fact, such feelings grow even stronger as you get older, and they are extremely motivating. As you mature, it may be more difficult to articulate your feelings without becoming self-conscious, which is an unfortunate reaction. But, your ability to explain your feelings isn't the issue. What is important is how they make you feel.

How many times have you heard successful people express a wish that a parent or mentor was still living, so that they could share a peak experience with them? My suggestion to anyone who has known such feelings is this: Keep past experiences alive—they will someday serve you well.

# Selling Yourself

There are few "naturals" in any business. Most sales professionals must take the time and effort to learn how best to deal with people. Is it sound procedure to become conscious of what the naturals do unconsciously—to learn the techniques that allow the less gifted to become skillful sales professionals through long and intelligent practice?

If you conclude that it is *not* sound procedure, then you throw overboard the value of all teaching and revert wholly to the trial-and-error school–which is all right, except that graduation is postponed to the brink of the grave. May you not assume that if you know some of the things that make selling effective for others, you can profit by playing some of the same strings yourself? This simple conclusion reflects common sense or clear thinking, and that is all that sales psychology really is—nothing high-brow, just good old-fashioned common sense. Looked at from that angle, selling psychology or strategy becomes less complicated and easier to put to work.

## Visualizing Strategies in Action

You have no doubt observed that, until they are told vividly, in language that they understand, many prospects fail to realize that they are not doing well for their business or their families. Similarly, many sales professionals do not realize that they are doing some things—or are not doing other things—that may mean much in sales won or lost.

The following prose endeavors to make you aware of some of the sales strategies that help sales professionals to win the liking and confidence of prospects, and to show you their application to your daily work. This is done largely through illustrative stories, incidents, and comments written in sales professionals' language. Visualize yourself using these principles in action.

Just being aware of some of these strategies may help you to become a better sales professional. The practices of others, adapted to your personality, should be profitable because successful and super successful sales professionals are using them every day.

## No Magic Shortcuts

"Strategy" does not imply shortcuts. There are no such things in selling as magic sales formulas or sales shortcuts—they are like the fountain of youth that Ponce de León, and others before and since, unsuccessfully sought as a shortcut to happiness. Forget any notions of gadgets and shortcuts. Consider instead the value of improving your sales technique, your knowledge of your business, and your knowledge of people. One top MDRT sales professional says that success varies in direct proportion to improvement in these factors.

Assuming *technical competence* in your business (the knowledge of what you have to sell; the knowledge of prospects' wants and needs; the knowledge of efficient selling methods, including the ability to discipline oneself; and a belief in your business and company), the principal factor in successful selling is a genuine desire for interaction with people. This gives power to your sales strategy and is the first step in the process of getting yourself believed in and accepted so that people will "think with you." In his book, *Influencing Human Behavior,* Harry Overstreet describes this concept as the supreme art.

## A Daily Lesson in Human Nature

Sales professionals need to continue to improve their imagination and their knowledge of people and how they behave. Getting new ideas and deepening their understanding of people enables them to make the strongest kind of individualized appeal. Fortunately, active sales professionals receive a daily lesson in human nature. They not only learn sales strategy at the fount of all such wisdom, but they apply the strategies learned from books and associates. Thus, they convert the best of strategies into habits of action that may enable them, in time, to become master sales professionals. It takes time to do that, just as it takes time to become a master of any art or science.

A sales professional can perhaps make a living by calling with automaton-like regularity on enough people, and delivering the same old rusty story in the same old dull way. But this is not selling, and the rewards are likely to be poor.

Perhaps too much emphasis has been put on hard work and the law of averages, important as these are. It is quite possible to be a hard worker who has great faith in the law of averages, and yet be a drone and a bore to the public. On the other hand, one can be skillful in gaining the confidence and interest of people, and yet be unable to summon enough self-discipline to ever attain a place among the leaders.

## Be Well-Rounded

Of all people in the various professions, sales professionals need to be well rounded. The average buyer is demanding a superior type of salesmanship. Now, as never before, sales professionals need to consider how they look and act when they are in public view. Let it never be said of them that they have to resort to any negative expedients as substitutes for finding definite needs and offering a definite plan to cover them.

## Prospects' Attitudes and Likes

If you have a tendency to put prospects down when you are unable to get to first base with them—perhaps following an unusually heavy day of rebuffs and turndowns in the field—remember that resistance is natural and that you must be prepared to overcome it.

Perhaps the fault lies with you. Don't blame prospects for lack of interest. This would be as unreasonable as a farmer's blaming an early frost on the thermometer. It's up to you to get prospects to like you and to be interested in what you have to offer.

An able sales professional in a small Wisconsin farming community tells about calling on a prosperous farmer who told him to come back the next week. For ten straight weeks, the farmer was always out. The eleventh week, the sales professional drove right into the barn. He narrates: "The prospect was slow in hiding and I caught him. I said, 'Are you afraid of me? You don't have to be. You don't have to buy my product if you don't want to. Let's go into the kitchen.' I could have gotten the sale for two cents, but I didn't tell him I knew it. Ma was in the kitchen. I said, 'I am going to have a heart-to-heart talk with you. Watch my eyes so that you can see I'm telling the truth.' " He told the story of his product, and three weeks later he had the farmer as his client.

A merchandising expert once said, "Every evident effort to sell creates corresponding resistance." People just don't like to be sold anything or to be interrupted, especially by strangers. They do not usually hide somewhere when they see you coming, but they erect other kinds of barriers, even a defensive mask that hides their natural selves, an artificial veneer that you may have to peel off to be successful.

It is natural for people to resist new things. Most worthwhile things that are part of your progress have been accomplished in spite of resistance. Back in the 1820s, railroads were opposed because, among other things, it was said that they would startle people and cause premature births among women, cattle, and hogs; cause cows to cease giving milk; and stop hens from laying. Today, though outwardly things have changed, human nature remains the same. People generally prefer not to have their inertia interrupted, so anticipate resistance.

## The Personal Element

Granting the value of good salesmanship in eliminating natural resistance, you must realize that the majority of sales, if your experience is typical, are made to people with whom you have some degree of acquaintanceship or friendship. For instance, in one group of sales professionals, all of whom produce $100,000 or more annually, over 40 percent of their average sales are made to people they have known for more than five years. About 70 percent of sales are made to people whom they have known for over one year.

Other studies have shown similar results. An able company vice president seems warranted in saying, "If you will analyze the production of sales professionals throughout the country who produce $150,000 of paid business upward each year, you will find that their sales activities indicate clearly that 85 percent of their individual sales come through channels in which the personal element plays an important part." That is, sales professionals are acquainted with prospects or with friends of prospects.

A program for becoming favorably known to people is of great importance and value to sales professionals. They need to convert strangers into friends, and if they can do it prior to the interview, so much the better. As one sales professional puts it, "Remember, no one fails in this business because they know too many people who like them. Every day, in every way, you must extend your 'friendship frontier.' The sales professionals' assistants are their friends, the people on their payroll without pay."

Fortunately, it is unnecessary to invest any great amount of money to increase one's acquaintances and friends. Membership in a congenial country club certainly does no harm, but many sales professionals say that their activity in organizations such as a church, civic societies, and community projects is really valuable and supplies contacts that are more lucrative than the social kind.

## What Prospects Ask Themselves

What are prospects apt to ask themselves when you call on them? Each prospect will have different questions, but enough is known about prospects' reactions to allow us to set down the most likely subconscious queries:

- ✓ Do I like this person? Does he/she click with me?
- ✓ Does this person know the business? Can I learn something that will be useful to me?
- ✓ Do I get a feeling of confidence about this person? Is this an honest sales professional?
- ✓ Will this person look at this matter from my point of view and give me an honest solution?

These questions could be asked in many different ways, but they all add up to the same thing. One MDRT sales professional in New York City says, "The prospect must immediately be made to feel that I am a competent and sincere person, well versed in the intricacies of my product or service, and anxious to help."

Sincerity and technical competence will carry sales professionals a considerable distance, even if they have an otherwise bland personality. A sales professional in the South, who is unattractive in appearance and manner, has built a fairly good business by admitting to prospects that he cannot compete with other sales professionals on the basis of personality or salesmanship, but his knowledge of the business and his service to clients help him to do the kind of job the prospect would want done. Through sheer sincerity and ability, this sales professional gets over most of the hurdles—not with grace and ease, but sufficiently well to illustrate how sincerity and a thorough knowledge of the product can build confidence.

One company asked its established sales professionals to list their 10 best clients. A letter was sent to each name on the various lists asking why the client had bought from this particular sales professional. The replies were exceedingly interesting, and they confirm the points made previously. The principal reasons, in order, were: friendship; good knowledge of the product; client's confidence in the seller; ability to make the client understand the product; no high-pressured approach; and good service.

## What Clients Like

Recently, a financial services company asked some of its clients why they were willing to recommend certain sales professionals to their friends. Here are some of the replies:

✓ A farmer said: "We farmers have been deceived so often by sales professionals of various kinds, I have always looked with a kind of suspicion on them until this sales professional came along. From the start, he made me feel he was trying to help me instead of making what he could out of me. I can trust him, so I recommend him to others and I know they will thank me, for he always does something good for people, whether he sells them insurance or not."

✓ A doctor said: "Until this sales professional came along, I looked at his product as a racket. He has shown me through the way he came to me, what he did for me, and what he continues to do for me, that his product can be practiced as a profession. Just as my professional function is to look after the physical health of my patients, his is to look after the financial health of his clients. Since all my friends need the service he renders, I suggest to them that they use him."

✓ A clerk said: "My sales professional taught me the value of saving and how to save. He had done a lot of work, planning a program for me and teaching me how to achieve financial success. I am so enthusiastic about my plan, I want my friends to have the same satisfaction. That is why I recommend him to others."

✓ A banker said: "My sales professional has the happy faculty of making his clients feel that he puts their interests first. He creates this impression because he is sincere, and renders a valuable, essential service. Because I knew something about banking, it does not follow that I knew his product. Therefore, I use a specialist."

✓ A manufacturer said: "Why shouldn't I recommend a sales professional who practically saved our business? Many years ago, through the recommendation of a friend of mine, I got this sales professional to study my insurance coverage and help me work out a program. He did a splendid job that resulted, among other things, in my paying back all the loans on my insurance, money I had borrowed to speculate with in the stock market. It did not mean a cent of income to him because he felt I had enough insurance. However, feeling that I wanted to reward him for his service to me and getting to love the fellow for what he was, I began to recommend him to different friends. Then I decided to have him make a study of our corporation insurance program. I would have had him do this before, but for the fact that the chairman of the board had a son who was a general insurance broker through whom we had bought over half a million dollars of corporation insurance. Well, he did a fine job, gave a copy of his report to each officer, and made certain suggestions that he knew would result not in business for him but for our brokers. He is an able, unselfish man, and I'll back him to the limit."

A new member of The Million Dollar Round Table received the following letter from one of his clients. Indirectly, it gives a big clue as to why this sales professional is a millionaire producer.

---

Dear [MDRT sales professional's name]:

In my experience, I have been called on by hundreds of solicitors; in fact, my own brother was a sales professional for an excellent company. During his lifetime he never sold me a thing—strange as it may seem.

I have an insurance policy that I took out some 30 years ago with probably the closest friend I ever had, and I still own it. During those years, as I said before, I have been called on by innumerable solicitors. I say to you with all sincerity that your method of approach inspires confidence and leads me to feel that, if I had met you in my younger days, I would have bought all my policies from you.

In my contact with you, I have always felt—and I do today—that your interests are with the prospect, for his benefit and not for the mere securing of a commission. I am positive in my mind that this has been the secret of your success. I only wish this letter could be published for the reference and guidance of sales professionals who feel they are especially qualified to handle this particular class of salesmanship, which I consider the highest form of salesmanship in the world.

---

Given this picture of the attitudes and likes of prospects and customers, what can be done to earn them? Let's examine the various contributing factors in the order of their impression on the prospect. You can endeavor to ensure a favorable first impression by giving attention to more or less mechanical matters, such as your appearance, speech, and actions. The next section concerns itself with the role of these factors in eliminating resistance and building acceptance.

## Ensuring a Favorable First Impression

One hot August morning, a steel sales professional entered the office of a manufacturing executive wearing yesterday's shirt and a baggy suit. A cigar was stuck in the corner of his mouth. Muttering his words, he said, "Good morning, sir. I represent the Albany Steel Company."

"You what?" said the prospect. "You *represent* Albany? Look here, young man, I know several Albany officials and you don't represent them—you *misrepresent* them. Good morning to you!"

An often-quoted statement of Ralph Waldo Emerson bears repeating here: "What you are speaks so loudly, I cannot hear what you say." In other words, the impression conveyed by your appearance, voice and speech, manner, attitude, and actions goes a long way toward giving the prospect an intimate character picture of you.

What kind of person do your prospects see when you appear before them? They get a series of second-splitting images or photographs of you, and they store the most important ones in their consciousness.

Some people say that an interview is made or broken in the first 10 seconds. Be that as it may, we do form snap judgments of people based on our impressions during the first few seconds of meeting them. If these judgments are bad, then any sale would be made in spite of a prospect's initial poor impression of the sales professional. On the other hand, a good impression is bound to help the sale and makes it unnecessary to fight an uphill battle against the prospect's unfavorable first impression.

## Look the Part

Does your attire, your manner, your voice tell your prospects that you are the kind of person they might be willing to do business with? When we see a sheep, we do not expect to discover that it is a wolf in sheep's clothing. We assume that it is a genuine sheep until indications prove otherwise. Thus, the well-dressed sales professional, looking the part of an able, honest, attractive personality, is assumed to have those characteristics, unless they are later found wanting. If you look the part, you've made a good start. Clothes do not make the person, but, by lowering resistance, they help a great deal to define a sales professional. If you always look the part, you will immediately remove an obstacle.

## The Little Things That Count

A widely experienced Nebraska manager says, "The other day, a man called to see me, dressed like a character in the famous old play called *The Morning After.* He started in with an exceptionally good sales presentation, but my mind wandered. I looked at his shoes, his trousers, and glanced at his shirt and tie. I spent most of the time thinking about why, if all the things that this sales professional said were true, he was dressed so shabbily.

"He told me how many orders he was securing, how many customers he had, and how they bought large quantities of the product. His personal appearance seemed to prove conclusively that what he was saying was not true. I did not buy because I had no confidence in his statements.

"In order to sell successfully, a sales professional must make a good impression. He or she must look the part. The sales professional must look success, talk success, and act success. It's the little things that count—they all contribute to the successful handling of a sales interview."

It is frequently said that a person is well dressed when you do not notice whether he or she is well dressed or poorly dressed. That statement is open to challenge. The average person is not well dressed, and, for that reason, do we not favorably notice the person who is really well groomed?

Very often, we do not notice the clothes of well-dressed people because we *expect* those people to be well dressed. We notice people who are poorly dressed because their clothes are loud in color and style or sloppy enough to be noticed. A well-dressed business person is several cuts above a common individual; a well-groomed appearance is part of being a sales professional, and only a stunning designer original would probably be noticed favorably by others.

The manager of a successful company in the South undoubtedly can attribute much of his success to his personal image. His appearance is perfect, without being objectionably so. Compared to his peers, he buys suits that are twice as good and he shops for clothes half as often; he doesn't allow the pressure of business to delay a needed trip to the barber shop, and his shoes are well shined. He is not too well dressed to talk to the lower-income-generating prospects; but his appearance makes him look—and feel!—perfectly at home in the offices of affluent prospects.

## Well Dressed versus Overdressed

To be conservative is to be safe. If you have an urge for Nile green shirts with purple stripes, repress it. The sales professionals in one company dislike doing any collaborative work with their manager because his loud shirts embarrass them. They don't want prospects to know they are associated with him. Little things can make vital differences.

The fawn waistcoat, the eyeglasses with a black ribbon, the race-track suit—some sales professionals have been guilty of these and more—are best put away for masquerade parties unless you want to be taken for a circus barker, a fake stock sales hustler, or a professional gambler.

If you have any doubts about your attire, get an opinion from a close friend, or go to a conservative clothing store that has prices within your means. Describe your objective, and ask for an analysis. As a person who meets all kinds of people every day, you need business suits that are conservative in their cut, colors, and design. If they fit well and are kept well pressed and spotless, you will be well dressed and not overdressed. One sales professional always wears plain white shirts because they are always safe. You'll be on the safe side by being somewhat old-fashioned in your choice of clothes, because many of your prospective clients, although they won't say so, will have conservative ideas regarding dress. Many of the "latest wrinkles" have been discarded before the more conservatively minded people have become accustomed to them.

A sales professional who represses any taste for novel and garish clothes has a smart strategy. If your individuality must be expressed, do it in nonprofessional channels.

Many sales professionals dress to match the people on whom they are going to call. It is difficult to draw up any rules, but, generally speaking, if you were going to call on a high bank official, you would naturally dress pretty conservatively. For calling on a younger person, a fashionable shirt might be permissible. When calling on a farmer, be neat but not dressed in the "derby manner." If you have any doubts, stick to the conservative side.

A sales professional in Ohio, in confirming the importance of such matters, added this thought in connection to selling to women: "They demand courtesy and a very neat personal appearance. I never call on women on a rainy day, when my shoes might be dull and the press of my suit not so good."

## Personal Neatness

For men, "Shine your shoes but not your fingernails" is good advice. No one is offended by well cared-for fingernails, but many people are negative toward nails that have obviously received the attention of a manicurist. Let them be neat and well trimmed but not too shiny. Many people, both men and women, consider buffed fingers effeminate.

A sales professional in New England no doubt has prototypes in many other localities; his fingernails look as though he has just finished changing the grease in the differential. He is consistently a member of his company's $100,000 club, and his usual production is in the neighborhood of a million dollars. But two prospective buyers discovered, in a chance conversation, that neither of them would ever buy from him, largely because of their reaction to the appearance of his fingernails. The number of prospects who feel the same way is anybody's guess. A word of constructive criticism from the sales professional's spouse or from the head of his company could have done him a world of good.

Another little detail is a haircut. Unruly hair is compatible with the art of painting but not of selling. And when you leave the barbershop, don't take it with you. Perfumed hair, by the standards of many people, might result in an undesired classification. The need for a careful shave is almost too obvious to mention. Don't ever forget that these little things actually do make a difference—often, a vital difference.

## Your Voice and Speech

What about your voice or your speech? One nationally known telephone company puts it this way: "If you could call yourself up, what would you hear? Simply your own voice and speech—your sole representative. You would hear yourself as others hear you. Would it please you? Would you know, in an instant, that here was a person genuinely courteous, interested, alert? Would there be something about your tone of voice, your way of greeting, your manners, the ease with which you were understood, which gave a glimpse of a friendly face, of an alert, capable person? Would you find yourself quickly responding to an attractive personality?

"Since your voice and speech are all that there is to your telephone personality, you'll want to study them and be thinking about using the 'voice with a smile' almost every time you make or answer a call. Then, too, you'll want to be careful about the clearness of your speech. If you speak distinctly, making it easy for the other person to understand, you will make a good impression from that one feature alone."

Careless speech is a real handicap. People who would write correctly are frequently exceedingly sloppy in their speech. "These kind" instead of "this kind" is not very serious, nor is "kind of a" instead of "kind of" going to do any great harm. But "it don't" for "it doesn't" and "between you and I" for "between you and me" rub many people the wrong way.

Ask someone to criticize your speech for such grammatical errors; at the same time, check yourself on slang. The following expressions are apt to give a very poor impression and should be eliminated from everyone's vocabulary—but particularly that of a sales professional whose livelihood depends on meeting people favorably:

"Listen"   "Y'understand?"

"See"   "You know what I mean?"

"Look"   "I'm telling ya"

"Huh?"   "I mean"

A sales professional in Tennessee says, "Y'understand?" after about every second sentence. It is an entirely unconscious habit, but it grates on people. It implies that there is some question whether the listener is intelligent enough to follow the line of thought. The unuttered answer to this sales professional's rhetorical question is: "What do you think? Do I appear a little dumb?"

When you speak, you deliver two messages. The first is in what you say, and the second is in how you say it. A masterful sentence can be spoken with a raspy voice, with an unenthusiastic yawn, with a gaze into space, with a mumble, with hesitations, and in countless other ways.

Reading aloud is one of the best ways to learn to speak distinctly and with expression. These qualities are lacking in a book sales professional's memorized spiel, and they're missing from your speech if you slide over words and talk in a monotone.

Many years ago, a well-known sales professional and author, R. C. Borden, stressed the importance of talking interestingly and correctly. Here are the six speaking principles he noted:

1. *Talk clearly.* Give each syllable its full value, accurately and distinctly. About 150 words a minute is the right average speed, for clearness. Don't let down in clearness by tagging on extra words at the end of a sentence.

2. *Talk conversationally.* A good speaker makes you say to yourself, "This speaker is no stuffed shirt, no demagogue. Instead, he or she is likable, level-headed, and trustworthy."

3. *Talk earnestly.* Every successful speaker has a "fire alarm" quality in his or her voice. Its intense earnestness makes your spine tingle. In the days of radio, that quality in an orator's voice was often vital. It was one of the factors, for instance, that enabled Winston Churchill to persuade his listeners during Britain's "finest hour."

4. *Talk animatedly.* To animate your voice, change your speed of delivery, vary your pitch, or alternate your volume. Franklin D. Roosevelt's delivery was like a sightseeing

bus; it sped up in unimportant territory, then slowed down when it passed points of special interest.

5. *Make your pauses punctuate.* When you pause after prepositions (with, to, for, at) and articles (the, a, an), your pauses mutilate. Every pause should have the value of a punctuation mark— a comma, semicolon, period, or question mark.

6. *Avoid "word whiskers."* Don't blemish your delivery with "er . . . " or nervous coughs. Avoid any speech mannerisms or gestures that detract attention from what you are saying.

## Shaking Hands

There are many other likes and dislikes to which alert sales professionals must pay heed. For instance, when you go into someone's office, do you extend your hand for a handshake? If you do, break yourself of the habit. Many people do not like to shake hands with people they don't know; some people even find it somewhat repulsive to shake hands with strangers. The safe guideline is: Don't shake hands unless the prospect initiates the gesture, or unless your prospect is a worker who might think that you are not shaking hands because his or her work status is too menial.

"It's easy," says one sales professional, "to tell whether prospects want to shake hands. Just watch for any movement of their right arm. You can do this while looking directly at them, just by being conscious of it."

You might have heard or read about the limp, clammy, obsequious handshake of Uriah Heep in Dickens's *David Copperfield.* Less attention has been given to the viselike grip and the pump-handle technique, both of which reflect the "personality-plus" school and are as obnoxious as the limp and languid shake. A commonsense, firm handshake is all that is needed, despite one sales professional's insistence that the real way to impress people is to extend the hand, palm up. When he shakes hands, it is an artificial shake. Don't be artificial; be natural.

One can scarcely find fault when you say, "May I sit down?" and then you sit. But wait until you are on a friendly basis before shaking hands.

You may never reach a friendly basis if you glance over at the mail or other private material on your prospects' desks. This common failing is usually done unconsciously. But it is always obvious to prospects, and they aren't apt to like it.

### Common Sense: A Good Leader

Most of your acceptable actions will rightly be based on common sense. You may have been advised to look the other person in the eye because a shifty gaze reveals a dishonest character. This advice has some merit, if applied with some finesse. Don't let it result in a staring-down process. Be reminded of an oil company advertisement many years ago, which begins with the sales professional talking.

"What are you staring at?" the sales professional is asked by the company president.

"I'm practicing salesmanship, sir," he answers, surprised.

"Well, I thought it was hypnotism," is the comeback.

What is the moral of all this? A favorable appearance, careful speech distinctly spoken, actions that people like—all are great resistance eliminators. They help you to win the liking and confidence of people. To be sure, they are mostly mechanical, but they are important in building a foundation for the more important attitudes and processes that are about to be discussed.

## The Selling Process

The selling process—the orderly progression that leads prospects to make certain buying decisions—is the framework on which your sales presentation is built. It guides and channels prospects' thinking so that they feel your product or service will provide the best solution to their problems. Its full impact is realized because of your concentration on the needs of your prospects. Your ability to state ideas in appropriate language provides effective *customer-oriented* communication that will guide sale after sale to a successful close.

Knowledgeable sales professionals use the various stages in the selling process to move customers' minds toward a favorable decision. This sequence of selling provides the framework within which you can make appeals to your customers' buying motives. It is imperative for you to understand how to apply the basic principles of this selling process by building a sales presentation that always emphasizes the wants and needs that are in your prospects' minds.

Attention, interest, desire, conviction, and action (the close)—these are the five stages through which every prospect's mind must pass before he or she decides to accept your sales presentation as solution-oriented with respect to his or her self-interests. To better understand each of these stages in the prospect's decision, a brief analysis of each is given below. Keep in mind always that *one stage fuses into the next.* We separate them here only to help you better understand the contribution of each to the buying process.

## Attention Stage

The positive approach of sales professionals secures the opportunity to indicate, as quickly as possible, the answer to the first buying decision prospects must make: "Why should I see this sales professional?" Sales professionals must try to convince prospects quickly that they have something of genuine advantage for their customers. They must make prospects want to hear the entire presentation. This stage is critical, for prospects' attention obviously must be secured if sales professionals are to have the opportunity to develop further interest in the product they have to offer.

The attention stage provides something else: the opportunity to test the accuracy of information secured in advance of your interview and also to learn any new facts that could not be secured prior to the interview. The information secured in your preapproach to prospects should have indicated: a need for your product or service, their authority to buy, and their eligibility (whether their credit status is acceptable for a large purchase). New facts may be revealed at this point. As you *listen,* your prospects may reveal further needs and wants.

## Interest Stage

Prospects' interests are strengthened as sales professionals, in an enthusiastic manner, move them along in the buying process and intensify the initial interest that was brought to light in the attention stage. This effort should make prospects want to hear more about the sales proposition.

You develop the knowledge that your prospects are not in the advantageous situation that they should be; you commence building on the foundation that your proposition will deal with their problems effectively. Your enthusiasm and pride in your product or service should further increase your prospects' confidence. You should whet their appetite by presenting a few specific selling points that indicate how what you offer can better serve their interests. The development of the interest stage is thus a part of the building process. Here's an example:

SALES PROFESSIONAL: "I came here because I believe that you, like all of us, want to reduce your home finance problems."

PROSPECT: "Yes, this is of interest to me, but I've been trying to reduce other expenses at this time."

SALES PROFESSIONAL: "The idea I want to present can result in substantial savings to you—probably thousands of dollars. I know that's of interest to you. Actually, I want to ask ..." [the sales professional then begins to move into the body of the presentation].

## Desire Stage

The desire for the sales professional's proposition is aroused in prospects' minds through persuasion and suggestion as they are moved to observe two things:

1. The disadvantages of their present situation—not having what the sales professional has to offer.
2. The advantages or profit to be gained by an acceptance of the sales professional's offer.

Typical dialogue might be:

SALES PROFESSIONAL: "Actually, my purpose in discussing your home financial problem is to permit you to deal with your other expense problems."
PROSPECT: "Well, I think I'm beginning to see that I've been ignoring one of my basic problems."

In this stage, a demonstration is used to highlight the definite advantage offered by your proposition. The demonstration arouses and heightens their desire and moves them toward conviction. Having gained prospects' interest and attention, you heighten their desire by hammering home product points that will satisfy their basic motivations. You appeal to their basic motivation, whether it is the need for love and affection or for performance and durability. Prospects will see the absolute relationship between your proposition and their own individual need or problem. Their desire is aroused when they realize what they are missing and what they can gain by accepting your product or service. In this phase of the sales presentation, an effort is made to stimulate prospects' senses—sight, hearing, touch, taste, and smell. Charts, graphs, pictures, photographs, advertisements, manuals, portfolios, models, samples and gifts, film and slides, testimonials, and other aids will be used to assist in the dramatization of the process.

## Conviction Stage

Conviction is secured when customers or prospects feel certain that claims made for the product or service are true and that it can satisfy their wants. Any questions or objections that have been raised will have been satisfactorily answered by the sales professionals. Through an effective demonstration and their responses to objections, the sales professionals will find themselves ready to secure confirmation from their customers. The demonstration answers any objections of the prospect because the sales professionals explain and prove, through evidence, the claims they have made for their proposition. Any old beliefs will have been changed or modified in terms of the proposition. It is essential that the demonstration accomplish this purpose completely and effectively if the sale is to progress to a close.

Always welcome the objections raised by your prospects; in dealing with them, you place yourself in a position to achieve your goal—the close of the sale. You will usually encounter objections during some phase of the selling process. Treat them as a normal part of the sales process, as opportunities to sell. (Why prospects object, when to answer their objections, the most common objections, and the techniques of answering them will be discussed in a separate chapter.)

SALES PROFESSIONAL: "If I can show you how we can devise a solution to your financial problems and start to move you toward financial security, would you. . . . "

PROSPECT: "Yes, if I was sure that I could afford it."

## The Close

The close is secured by moving prospects to make positive decisions because you are providing the best solution available to them. Desire and conviction on the prospects' part are converted into action. This is the sole objective of every sales presentation.

This is your prospect's last important decision. The moment of truth arrives when he or she says, "I want your offer and I want it now." Contrary to what many believe, the close actually starts in the very first stage of the buying sequence—it is not something separate and distinct from the sales presentation. For the close to be effective, all the other stages in the sequence of selling must have been successfully completed. There is no "secret" or "magic" to the close. It results only because a logical and effective sequence, coupled with honest persuasion, was established. The only basis for closing a sale is that your product or service provides the best solution to your prospects' needs.

The Marketing Science Institute study on the process of decision making—or the behavior that leads to a purchase decision—indicates the existence of not just one decision, but a "sequence of information acquisition and decision-making instances."

## Two Basic Questions

You should be asking yourself two important questions as you study the various stages in the buying process:

1. Do I have to take the prospect or customer though all the stages in the buying process before making my presentation?

2. If not, at which stage should I start my presentation?

The first question is quickly answered: You do not. *Experience* will provide the best answer to the second question, but you can learn from the techniques used by experienced sales professionals. They know that another sales professional may have taken the prospect through the various stages before their visit. If preapproach efforts do not provide the answer, the sales professional can determine how far the customer has progressed in the buying process with judicious questioning and attentive listening.

If prospects are in the desire stage, direct your efforts to the conviction stage and then endeavor to move toward a close. If you find that their interest and attention have already been developed, move them through the desire, conviction, and action stages. If the conviction stage has been reached, present product information and buying motivations that will convince them that your product is the best solution and will then move them to action. Your first problem is *always* to find out how far the prospect has progressed in the buying process. Then carry their minds from that stage to the close.

## A Final Touch

The final touch in the sequence of selling is often forgotten. It's the sixth step—the building of goodwill. Always remember to provide your customers with additional reinforcement of the wisdom of their decision. You will increase their confidence in you and in the company you represent; you will help them avoid "after-sale doubts"; and, even if the sale is not consummated at the moment, you will be laying the groundwork for a close in the near future. Finally, you will be building a most valuable intangible asset—the goodwill that is the foundation of a permanent business relationship.

Your complete presentation, based on an understanding of the buying process, should be given in an informal and warm manner. Certain segments of the sales presentation's content should be memorized. Do everything you can to ensure completeness and accuracy, and to avoid needless repetition. Always be guided by this basic truth: Everything you say is related to the specific interests of your customer.

The presentation that follows illustrates many of the points already discussed. It is placed here to provide you with a "feel" for how sales professionals ferret out significant facts about prospects and their companies. Good sales professionals will develop a complete presentation using the information obtained and their own product knowledge. The basic sequence of selling is followed in the example. Note especially that savvy sales professionals discover the vital facts about the particular organization and the prospects they are interviewing, and then build the entire presentation on these and on their thorough knowledge of their own product. Note also the skillful and tactful use of other companies' names in the closing phase. Background information and commentary are provided within the presentation itself.

The sample sales interview will introduce a sales professional who sells to business firms of all descriptions. On this call to a business associate, the sales professional will be making a sales presentation relating to the protection of business records.

To fully appreciate this actual interview, it is important to know some of the background facts and thinking that are in the mind of the sales professional.

This sales professional knows that every business has certain key records—accounts receivable, inventory, general ledger, minute books, tax records—that are essential to the smooth continuation of the business. These key records would have to be available after a fire, in order to obtain full recovery of losses from a fire insurance company, since each policy states that key business records must be available for the insurance company's examination. A company must be able to provide proof of its losses—which means the safety of its records is essential.

The sales professional also knows that surveys have proved that 43 percent of all firms that have lost their records in a fire have gone out of business within six months. Although this figure may seem startling, it is understandable. Without key records, a business cannot prove exactly who owes it money; the amount it owes creditors; how much inventory it had; why it was justified in taking certain tax exemptions; who its customers and suppliers are, and so on. Business is built on records. Without them, paralysis can result!

The sales professional is aware that fire is an unpredictable hazard and that it is the most common disaster that businesses face. He knows that the number-one cause of fire in the United States is smoking and matches, and the second biggest cause of fire is defective electrical wiring. As a result, the sales professional understands that no matter where a business is located and regardless of how "fireproof" a building is said to be, a fire can start, and some of the hottest, most disastrous fires have been in buildings thought to be "fireproof."

This sales professional understands that many prospects already have one or more safes for their key records. But he knows that a very large number of the safes being used to protect records from fire are not fire-safe. In addition to being old and giving uncertain protection from fire, many old safes are much heavier than modern safes. A safe can actually explode in a fire, because of the gases that old-type insulation generates. Old safes lack a modern look and therefore are out of place in a modern office—and, they take up more space than modern safes do. Old safes have small and inflexible interior capacity compared to a modern record safe with its flexible interior arrangement and large space for records.

In the sales interview that follows, observe the sales professional's great conviction and service attitude. You can understand why the sales professional feels deeply that his appointment may be the most important one his prospect ever has—the sales professional's product may one day save his prospect's business from destruction.

## Setting the Scene

This is an initial canvass call, by a sales professional, on the treasurer of a small, but growing manufacturer of furniture. The sales professional does not know exactly what records are important to this firm, although he can anticipate a list in a general way. Regarding the fire hazards, he can see that the offices where the records are located are in a fairly new brick building that is attached to a manufacturing plant of similar construction. Some of the furniture is made of wood, which would burn. Empty packing boxes and filled boxes ready for shipment are visible as he approaches the main entrance of the building; therefore, he knows that this business has fairly high potential for a fire and, given the brick construction, which retains the heat of a fire, the fire could be severe. Further, he knows that people smoke on the job and that the machinery present is electrically wired for the manufacturing processes. What kind of safe is currently in use, or what key records are needed to stay in business, the sales professional does not know. This information he will have to find out from the prospect.

We join the sales professional, Eric Stebbins, for the sales interview as he greets the company's treasurer, Donald Swanson.

SALES PROFESSIONAL: "How do you do, Mr. Swanson. I'm Eric Stebbins of the Maglio Safe Company."

TREASURER: "Glad to meet you, Mr. Stebbins. Won't you have a seat? What can I do for you?"

SALES PROFESSIONAL: "I'm very pleased to have this opportunity to speak to you, Mr. Swanson. I feel that I can be helpful to you as the treasurer of this company. As a security specialist in the protection of essential business records, I have been able to offer a number of helpful suggestions to quite a few businesses in town. I'm wondering, Mr. Swanson: How long has your firm been in business?"

[The sales professional realizes he has talked long enough and needs to get Swanson into the discussion. By determining how long the firm has been in business, he can point out later the years of labor that will be lost if the firm fails because its records are destroyed in a fire. Swanson will probably want to answer this question since it's about his business.]

TREASURER: "We started in 1971. Had some rough years and then really blossomed out."

SALES PROFESSIONAL: "You sound very proud of your firm's success—and rightly so. In my work with Maglio Safe, I have had the opportunity to serve many firms that started small and gradually grew big. It's very satisfying. As record protection specialists, we have found that many firms have some key records in common, and others have essential business records that are almost unique to their firm or type of business. If you had to select the most essential records you have, what would you name as number one? Accounts receivable?"

TREASURER: "Yes, I guess they would be number one."

SALES PROFESSIONAL: "I'm curious, Mr. Swanson: How do you sell your furniture—through dealers?"

TREASURER: "Yes, all of our sales are through direct retail dealers in all parts of the country."

SALES PROFESSIONAL: "I assume, then, that you have to maintain an inventory and records to show you what you have on hand. Is that right?"

TREASURER: "Yes."

SALES PROFESSIONAL: "Then it might be disturbing and perhaps disastrous if you lost your inventory records? In a fire, for example?"

TREASURER: "Yes, I suppose so, but we have fire insurance. That should cover us."

[Although most businesses have fire insurance today, this had to be definitely established. Swanson volunteered it! He probably doesn't realize that "proof of loss" is required in his fire policy.]

SALES PROFESSIONAL: "Have you ever put in a claim against your fire insurance policy?"

TREASURER: "No, not yet, thank goodness!"

SALES PROFESSIONAL: "I have a sample policy here which points out clearly that, in case of loss, records would have to be made available to the fire insurance company, so they could prove the amount of the loss. Then, earlier in the policy, it states that these key records are not covered by the policy. You told me that accounts receivable and inventory records and some others are extremely important to you. Where do you house these records at night?"

[At this point, the sales professional knows that this firm has key records and that someone thought enough about the possibility of fire to buy fire insurance. But how these records are protected has not been established. Even if the company has one good safe, it could use a small one for each key executive or department head—or anyone who may have some vital records needed for full fire insurance recovery. Almost definitely, each key person has records to keep a particular part of the company going. These would be needed more than ever after a fire.]

TREASURER: "We keep our most important records in a big safe in the next office, where most of our accounting work is done."

SALES PROFESSIONAL: "Since record protection is my field, Mr. Swanson, I may be able to offer some suggestions on the protection of these records—things I've learned while working with other companies. [Getting up.] Why don't we take a look at your safe and accounting office?"

TREASURER: [Getting up.] "I guess so."

[The sales professional first examines the safe carefully, without speaking. He measures the outside and inside dimensions, makes a quick sketch of the interior of the safe, checks the outside walls and door of the safe, and the inside of the door. He runs his fingers along the bottom of the doorjamb. He finds white powder along the doorjamb. He writes down the serial number, which appears on a metal label. No other label can be found. He knows from experience that the safe is about 60 years old and should not be used to protect vital records. During this period of about one minute, he does not speak with Swanson—he just carefully surveys the safe.]

SALES PROFESSIONAL: "Very interesting, Mr. Swanson! This safe is much older than your company. Did you buy it second-hand, or was it left by the previous tenant of this building?"

TREASURER: "It was purchased from someone else who was going out of business; I don't remember exactly."

SALES PROFESSIONAL: "I see. Based on my company's knowledge of safes of all types, we would estimate this safe to be at least 60 years old. That would mean it was manufactured in about 1939—just before World War II. It was a fine safe in its day—and it certainly looks strong even today. Since you are depending on the ability of this safe to prevent the heat of a fire from destroying your key records, naturally you ought to know where you stand. If you're putting too much trust in this safe, I'm sure you'd want to know, wouldn't you, Mr. Swanson?"

[The sales professional wants to be sure that Swanson is attentive to what he is going to say now. Stebbins knows that key records are kept here and that the safe has outlived its usefulness and definitely should not be trusted with important records. If he can convince Swanson of the danger and awkwardness of his old safe, as well as other disadvantages, he may be able to obtain approval for a new, modern Maglio safe. Let's see how Stebbins develops this.]

TREASURER: "Of course I want to know if that's true."

SALES PROFESSIONAL: "Well, Mr. Swanson, I appreciate that it's easy for someone who does not know the facts to tell you that, just because something is old, it is not good. But what I am going to say comes from the experience of my company. As you probably know, we have been in business more than 100 years. We built the safe that protects the Constitution of the United States from fire. First of all, Mr. Swanson, the purpose of a record safe is obviously to protect records. Paper will char and turn to ashes at approximately 350 degrees Fahrenheit. You have a refrigerator at home, don't you, Mr. Swanson?"

TREASURER: "Why, of course!"

SALES PROFESSIONAL: "Well, the purpose of your refrigerator is to keep the temperature inside below the spoiling point of your food. Isn't that right?"

TREASURER: "Naturally."

SALES PROFESSIONAL: "A safe for your records must do the same thing. If the construction of the safe allowed heat to penetrate so that the temperature rose to about 350 degrees Fahrenheit, then your records would be destroyed. If your refrigerator let your food spoil, you wouldn't be too happy, would you? Of course not! Then the question is: Would the safe you now have keep out most of the heat during a fire? Would the inside stay below 350 degrees Fahrenheit? One place where heat could enter quickly is the doorjambs— where the door and the body jambs come together, as you can see on this drawing and [pointing out on the old safe] as you can see here on your present safe. You can see for yourself just how large an open space there is on your present safe. As I open the door of your safe, you can see that this open space continues right straight into the interior of this old safe. Can you see that, Mr. Swanson?"

TREASURER: "Yes, I can!"

SALES PROFESSIONAL: "Another consideration in keeping heat out is the walls of your safe. Naturally, you have two side walls, a back wall, a top, and a bottom. As you can observe, the safe was made of a metal inner shell such as this [sketching on a pad] and an outer metal shell. In between these two shells was poured common cement. As the heat of a fire surrounds your safe, the heat attempts to penetrate the sides of the safe. This cement is all that can prevent the heat from getting inside. You've seen grass or weeds grow through a crack in a sidewalk, haven't you, Mr. Swanson?"

TREASURER: "Oh, yes."

SALES PROFESSIONAL: "Naturally, to make cement in the first place, you must have water. But after a period of years, this water is free to evaporate. That's what happens with the concrete in old safes. You may have noticed the powder on the bottom of the jamb of your safe, right here [gathering some in his hand to show Swanson]. This is the dried-out cement insulation powdering out of the walls and door of your safe. You may wonder why anyone was able to manufacture a safe this way, knowing all these facts. Did that occur to you, Mr. Swanson?"

TREASURER: "I suppose it did."

SALES PROFESSIONAL: "The truth is that 60 years ago there was no reliable way known for pretesting the ability of a safe to protect its records from heat destruction. Today, each model of our Maglio record safes is tested and certified by the Underwriters' Laboratories in Chicago. This furnishes the public with a consumer's guarantee for record protection."

[Naturally, Stebbins can't continue to tear down Swanson's old unsafe safe without substituting a more modern, reliable safe to take its place. The sales professional knows his prospect has a problem; now, he must be certain Swanson recognizes that problem. If Swanson agrees, Stebbins can go on and try to convince him that a new, trustworthy Maglio record safe is the solution— and get him to accept this solution at once, if at all possible. Tomorrow could be one day too late.]

SALES PROFESSIONAL: "I've covered quite a few points, Mr. Swanson. I did want to ask you if you're familiar with the Underwriters' Laboratories that tests electrical equipment and many household items for fire safety. Do you know of the Underwriters' Laboratories?"

[Since Stebbins is using UL as a third-person expert, so he wants to be sure Swanson regards it as expert testimony.]

TREASURER: "Oh, yes, we have UL tags on some of our machinery."

SALES PROFESSIONAL: "Can you understand why your old safe looks strong, but is a substantial risk for protecting records?"

TREASURER: "Now I think I can see that."

SALES PROFESSIONAL: "Perhaps I can make it even clearer by showing you a picture of a modern Maglio record safe for comparison. Here is a view of the safe closed. You can see at once how much more modern it is."

[The sales professional presents his solution for the first time, sliding smoothly from Swanson's last statement.]

SALES PROFESSIONAL: "Now on this page is an inside view showing the interior arrangement of one style. Actually, a modern Maglio can be arranged with almost any kind of interior units a business may need—confidential lockers, shelves that pull out for machine accounting records, cash drawers, handy document files—just another something to make the interior of the safe fit the needs and whims of the people who use it. And if you wish to change the locations of these units or add others later, it can be done in a matter of minutes with just a screwdriver. Of course, one of the limitations of old-style safes like yours is the permanent, inflexible interior that it came with."

[Swanson is still listening and watching. He may have reservations, but he isn't stopping the presentation. Stebbins has stopped along the way to ask questions, giving Swanson a chance to talk and raise objections. Stebbins must now assume Swanson is at least interested in hearing him through, but the sales professional must get specific on his alternative.]

SALES PROFESSIONAL: "Based on the measurements of your present safe, you have 40 inches of height inside, 18 inches of width, and 15 inches of depth. Since you keep your accounts receivable ledgers and inventory record cards in the safe, I'm wondering: What other important records do you keep in your present safe at night?"

TREASURER: "We keep our general ledger and tax records. That's about all."

SALES PROFESSIONAL: "Since you are a corporation, where do you keep your corporate minutes books?"

TREASURER: "I keep those locked up in my desk."

SALES PROFESSIONAL: "Are there any other records you would hate to lose that are not kept in the safe at night?"

TREASURER: "No, that's all!"

SALES PROFESSIONAL: "From experience with many corporations, we have found they are so afraid of having their minutes books destroyed or seen by unauthorized personnel that they keep them in a locked compartment in the record safe. Perhaps we can make a suggestion that could give your company the same security. By the way, I meant to ask you earlier: What monetary value would you put on your accounts receivable? What would you estimate?"

TREASURER: "I'd rather not divulge that."

[This may be important when the price of the new safe is revealed. If the company's value is a million dollars, spending $2,000 to protect this amount would certainly not be unreasonable.]

SALES PROFESSIONAL: "I assure you, Mr. Swanson, that our conversation is confidential. An estimate is all that I need. Would you say they are worth $500,000?"

TREASURER: "Considerably more than that!"

[Stebbins has his estimate, which is all he needs.]

SALES PROFESSIONAL: "More than $500,000, then. As the treasurer of your company, you would be responsible, as in most companies, wouldn't you, if for any reason these accounts receivable and others records were lost?"

[Stebbins obviously knows that this is true, but he wants Swanson to acknowledge openly his responsibility for the protection of the key records.]

TREASURER: "Why, yes, I suppose I would be responsible."

SALES PROFESSIONAL: "In that case, since we agreed earlier that your present safe was the best available in its day, I cannot honestly recommend that you trust it for the safekeeping of your records any longer. After my visit with you and my examination of your method of record protection today, I would be completely negligent if I did not advise you of this hazard. As the treasurer of this growing company, and with, let us say, more than $500,000 in accounts receivable, which could be disastrous if lost, I would like to make a suggestion to you, on behalf of the Maglio Safe Company. In place of your present untested safe, we would recommend a modern Maglio record safe. Based on the volume of your vital records, the model you need would take up less floor space, but would give you more capacity—some extra room so your company could keep growing without outgrowing the safe."

[Stebbins takes out an order form to get Swanson used to seeing it.]

SALES PROFESSIONAL: "Just to show you what this would look like inside [sketching interior layout], this modern record safe would provide you with a locker, key-locked, up in the top of the safe for your personal confidential records, including your minutes books; your accounts receivable ledgers would go on two shelves here; and your inventory record cards would be placed in drawers just below the center of the safe here. Your tax records, since they are also very confidential, could be placed in a key-locked locker below that. This would leave you about ten percent of unassigned space at the bottom—for expansion, as records are added in the future. [Pause.] Does that cover everything?"

TREASURER: "Yes, it seems to."

SALES PROFESSIONAL: "May I stress again that this interior arrangement can be quickly and easily changed as you may wish in the future. Also, as the treasurer, you will be interested in another security feature of this modern Maglio. In place of the old-style combination lock with the numbers facing out, we have an exclusive Counterspy combination dial where the numbers are on the top, facing up. This way, only the person who is authorized to know the combination can see the numbers. They are kept away from prying eyes."

[Stebbins quickly fills out the order form to show prices, but leaves out details to be added later, when time permits.]

SALES PROFESSIONAL: "That completes my company's recommendation to your firm, Mr. Swanson. After considering the risk you are taking, as a company and personally, don't you feel it would be wise to replace your old safe with the modern Maglio record safe we are suggesting—just as the Pillsbury Company and Sloan Walters have done?"

TREASURER: "Of course we've had our old safe for a long time. It's like a part of us!"

SALES PROFESSIONAL: "We appreciate that, Mr. Swanson. But the main reason for having a safe is to keep your records safe. Fortunately, you haven't had a fire yet. If you have a fire this week, we're just afraid your old safe won't turn out to be such a good friend."

TREASURER: "We haven't had a fire, either, and we take good safety precautions to avoid one."

SALES PROFESSIONAL: "I'm glad you do, Mr. Swanson. We don't want you to have a fire. If you did, however, it would be the responsibility of our Maglio safe to protect the records you'd need after a fire—just as we protect the Constitution. I'm sure you realize that you could have a fire, Mr. Swanson; otherwise, you'd cancel your fire insurance. And I'm certain you agree your records are a crucial part of your business, don't you, Mr. Swanson?"

TREASURER: "Well . . . yes."

SALES PROFESSIONAL: "You know by now just how big a gamble your old safe really is, and that all you have now to protect your records from destruction by heat is that safe. Don't you agree it would be cheaper to get a modern Maglio record safe you could trust, rather than risk the collapse of your business by losing your records?"

TREASURER: "Maybe it would, but right now a new safe would cost more than we can really afford. We are trying to economize. I think we ought to wait."

SALES PROFESSIONAL: "The Maglio safe that will do the job for you, Mr. Swanson, will cost you less than $9.75 per month during the next 20 years. When you consider the amount of money you have spent to get a half-million dollars in accounts receivable on your books, and what would happen to you and your company if you lost them suddenly, $9.75 per month is a real bargain. If you wait, it may cost you more than a million dollars—maybe your entire business!"

TREASURER: "What's the full amount?"

SALES PROFESSIONAL: "Just $2,340, including the flexible interior arrangement."

[Stebbins has been closing strongly for some time now. Swanson needs this protection at once. Stebbins can only render a service if he continues to persuade Swanson to take action right now. Swanson continues to listen; he must be turning over the pros and cons in his mind. A little more reassurance and he may sign.]

SALES PROFESSIONAL: "If you decide now to rid yourself of this hazard, you'll never regret it, Mr. Swanson. It is your responsibility as treasurer, and you know you can put your trust in our Maglio safe. As a businessperson, you certainly should be willing to protect the big investment you have in your vital accounts receivable, inventory records, plus all the other key records you must have to stay in business!"

[Places the order form directly before Swanson.]

SALES PROFESSIONAL: "There's little to be gained by waiting, and so much is at risk. I've given you all the facts. We will get you this protection right away, Mr. Swanson, if you'll give me your OK right here. It's the right decision."

[With this, he places his pen before Swanson to sign the sales order.]

TREASURER: "I guess you're right. I wish we didn't have to spend the money, but I'd hate to lose our records." [He signs the sale order.]

SALES PROFESSIONAL: "You're making the right decision. It's a fine investment!"

## Customers Are Individuals

Treat each customer as an individual personality. Never classify prospects as definite types. Despite attempts to classify customers as a limited number of definite types in order to simplify sales professionals' problems, no such effort has ever succeeded. Not only are all prospects *individuals,* but thcy are also capable of many moods and attitudes. You will probably find, from experience, that customers' moods may change a few times as your sales presentation progresses. This requires flexibility on your part. Adapt your personality and approach to customers and their present attitudes.

Once again, however, a question comes to mind: If customers should not be classified by types, is there any other way in which we can effect a classification that has real significance and will assist the sales profession in the selling situation? There is a positive answer to this question: Customers can and should be grouped on the basis of their buying problems. When you learn to serve customers in terms of their buying problems, you can give them valuable assistance in making wise decisions.

This "classification" technique works as follows. Find out, as quickly as possible, the type of buying problem your customers have. Do this by carefully listening to their responses. Then, to help them satisfy this problem, give an intelligent sales presentation tailored to the personal attitudes or moods that they reflect.

# Chapter 2

# Selling Ideas

Y ou have now entered the heart of this book, the chapters that offer ideas fro.. :/1DRT members on almost every conceivable aspect of selling: getting an interview, uncovering facts and motivations, selling to individuals, selling to businesses, selling to various markets, and more.

Each entry, whether brief or substantial, offers sound and proven advice from the very best MDRT sales professionals.

## Obtaining the Interview

Securing interviews with prospects to whom you can tell your sales story requires additional planning and an understanding of several elements that are critical to the selling situation. Besides your product knowledge and your list of prospects, you must know how to obtain an interview with "the right prospects"; be prepared to capture their attention and develop their interest rapidly; and sustain their attention and interest as your presentation unfolds. When these objectives have been successfully accomplished, you can stimulate your prospects' desire with benefit-packed demonstrations and secure conviction. You can then close the sale. The realization of these goals is discussed in this chapter.

The initial interview will vary with the type of buyer, the product sold, and the reputation of the selling company. You will find that some business executives are more difficult to see because they are surrounded by subordinates whose duty it is to screen calls. This can occur particularly if you are selling an intangible or a specialty; it happens far less frequently to the sales professionals who call on wholesalers, retailers, and purchasing agents, a substantial part of whose work it is to interview sales professionals. A very great number of companies require that purchasing agents and buyers have assigned time periods for receiving and interviewing sales professionals.

In all selling situations, you should realize that there is no justification for the use of anything but an honest approach in arranging and securing interviews. Subterfuge or deception in this effort will most often result in resentment toward you. Many sales professionals overemphasize the difficulties of getting to see prospects. Your own experience will show you that interviews are often yours merely for the asking.

Some basic methods and suggestions can assist you in gaining interviews. A positive and confident attitude can overcome resistance in many situations. First, show respect for administrative assistants, receptionists, or junior employees. Their goodwill is an asset in securing cooperation. Your actions should reflect a *friendly* but *not familiar* attitude. Any questions asked of you should be answered in a straightforward manner. Sometimes, it may be appropriate to explain what you have to offer; you may wish to outline some of the benefits to be derived from your product or service. Sales professionals sometimes forget that a desirable personal impression is simply the result of an honest effort to secure cooperation. If you are forced to wait for your prospects or customers, use your "wait time" to good advantage by working on memoranda or reports, studying material pertaining to your product, or reading business and trade literature.

In requesting interviews, you may use one of the following approaches:

✓ "Will you please tell [Prospect's Name] that [Your Name] is here?"

✓ "Would you be kind enough to tell [Prospect's Name] that [Your Name] is here to see [him/her] about a business matter?"

✓ "Good afternoon; I would greatly appreciate your arranging an interview with [Prospect's Name] for me."

If an interview cannot be arranged immediately, say:

✓ "If it is not convenient for [Prospect's Name] to see me now, I would be glad to return later in the afternoon."

There are two important considerations for this aspect of the interview: (1) be certain that you are seeing the right prospect, and (2) limit the amount of time you wait to see any potential client, unless the distance you have come and the circumstances surrounding the interview dictate otherwise. Time is your most precious commodity. Always convey the impression that your time is valuable. In some instances, you may find that you are able to make other calls in the general area and return later. Whenever feasible, make advance appointments to limit "wait time."

Referrals, whether by telephone, a letter of introduction, or a brief note on one of your calling cards, will sometimes facilitate the securing of an interview.

In giving your own name, it is good practice to use the following technique: Rather than simply saying, for example, "My name is Jeananne McMahon," tell the prospect, "My name is McMahon, Jeananne McMahon." This gives you two chances, instead of just one, to impress your name in the prospect's mind.

Use of the telephone for finding prospects has been briefly mentioned. Now you will see how experienced sales professionals arrange appointments with the "right individuals." You will also learn how a telephone conversation can be used to separate a suspect from a prospect. Many years ago, an MDRT associate wrote a blueprint for achieving success via the telephone. Its advice is just as timely today as when it was originally written.

## Introduction via Telephone

You are a sales professional and you want to talk to ideal prospects because they are the buyers whom you have to see to make a sale. So you telephone for appointments. It's the logical thing to do. You have a product your ideal prospects need. A minimum of selling by you should make prospects realize that they will benefit from knowing more of the details.

But you can't talk to your ideal prospects directly. Assistants or secretaries are assigned to screen calls. What's the most direct way to get to talk with your ideal prospects? The following question-and-answer interview with a top-notch sales professional contains several how-to-do-it tips.

Q: "How do you start?"

A: "First, know your ideal prospect's name."

Q: "An obvious first thing. Suppose you don't have it."

A: "If you don't have it, get it from the telephone operator, *not* the assistant."

Q: "You've got it. Then what?"

A: "Well, let's say her name is Lynne Smith. When the assistant answers, just say, 'Ms. Smith, please, [Your Name] calling.' Say it confidently, and don't say it in the form of a question."

Q: "What do you mean?"

A: "Well, let's suppose you say, 'Is Ms. Smith there?' Number one, you indicate that you are not sure she is. Number two, you are not really asking to talk to Ms. Smith. You're asking if she is available. That's something entirely different. When you find out she is in, you then have to ask to talk to her. You're right back where you started. The question invites a protective 'No' and possibly a complete turndown."

Q: "What's your recommendation?"

A: "I always find it helpful, before I make a call, to visualize Ms. Smith as a friend of mine. It's then easy to imagine that it would be silly for me to telephone this friend of mine and expect her assistant or secretary to keep me from talking to her. So I'd say, 'Ms. Smith, please. This is [Name].' And, nine out of ten, she will pick up the phone a second later."

Q: "Why not just, 'Ms. Smith, please?' "

A: "Try that sometime, and find out for yourself. I give my name too, because whenever I forget, most assistants will ask who's calling. Then you have to tell them. The next question is usually, 'What company?' If you give the name of the company you're with, more than likely the assistant will ask you what it is all about."

Q: "You mean you *never* get into that kind of situation?"

A: "Don't misunderstand me. What I've said works most of the time."

Q: "What do you do for the other times?"

A: "Well, the worst thing you can do is to hedge. The best answer is: 'The [Name Company]; is she there?' You can see that leaves Ms. Smith's assistant with three choices: to plug you in, to tell you that she really isn't there, or to get into more discussion. If she is busy, and most times she is, the easiest thing for her to do is to put you through."

Q: "Is that all there is to it?"

A: "No. In many cases, an assistant will ask what you want to talk to Ms. Smith about. Hemming and hawing can kill the sale before it starts. Because while you are hemming, the assistant is thinking of a way to give you the brush-off."

Q: "What then"

A: "I try to duck that question and ask for the appointment again. I might say, 'Is this her assistant? I'm calling to make an appointment. Do you arrange Ms. Smith's appointments or shall I talk to her directly?'"

Q: "But suppose the assistant still resists?"

A: "Tell the assistant in the shortest, most direct fashion. Give assurance that your call will take but a moment. And wind up by asking to talk to your prospect."

Q: "Let's assume the assistant insists Ms. Smith is too busy to see you and tries to get you to talk to someone else . . . ."

A: "The best way to handle that is to tell the assistant you appreciate how valuable Ms. Smith's time is and that you'll be delighted to talk with her subordinate. But only if that person can approve a purchase. If it's Ms. Smith you *must* see, the best thing to do is backtrack. In that case, I would say, 'I'll be delighted to talk to her subordinate after I communicate with Ms. Smith. There's no urgency about this matter today. When would you suggest I call?'"

Q: "And then you get your chance to speak to Ms. Smith?"

A: "Usually, I do . . . ."

In addition to these suggestions for obtaining interviews, some other techniques can be used to assist in accomplishing this first objective. These include the use of advance communication and the intelligent employment of a business card. When you are trying to obtain interviews with prospects for the first time—especially in cold canvassing situations—one of three devices might pave the way for you: (1) an advance letter that is skillfully and interestingly written, (2) a postcard that carries an informative message, or (3) a business card or some type of advertising material that stimulates your prospects' interest.

**1.** An advance letter, written in easy-to-understand sentences that convey its purpose succinctly and with imagination and originality, may effectively introduce sales professionals and their propositions to prospects. Frequently, the letter is accompanied by a postcard on which prospects may indicate the time and date that would be most convenient for you to call. When you make the call, reference to the mailed communications gives you some common ground on which to initiate your opening remarks.

**2.** A postcard alone is used in somewhat the same fashion. The message it contains will necessarily be brief, but it achieves the basic purpose of announcing your impending visit. Various types of advertising material—booklets, broadsides, stuffers, folders, and catalogues—can also provide advance information about yourself, your company, and the products or services that you offer. They can be extremely helpful in easing a sales professional's first approach to a prospect. Here again, by referring to your advance advertising material, you provide a basis for discussion.

**3.** A business card also serves as an introduction if it is properly and creatively used. Be aware that some companies insist that a card be sent in before a sales professional will be received, and you must comply with the request. The card alone can be an asset when the prospect is already familiar with and impressed by your company. When an advance card is not required, most experienced sales professionals have found that the best time to employ the printed card is at the conclusion of an interview. It then becomes a source of reference for the interested prospect or customer. Some sales professionals have used the business card successfully with a more personal approach. They add a personal message—written on the card by hand—to capture the recipient's attention or curiosity when it is delivered.

## Capturing Your Prospects' Undivided Attention

You are now face-to-face with a prospect. In this *attention stage,* the prospect must make the first mental decision: "I have met this sales professional. Now why should I listen to his or her story?" Convince the prospect quickly that your products or services can be of genuine advantage. The opening statements you make and the impression you create must result in a positive response. Your entire effort here, and in all the other stages of the selling process, must be directed to securing genuine confidence on the part of the prospect. When this has been done, you are in a position to complete your sales presentation.

Novice sales professionals often ask: "Does this mean that after a brief introduction of myself and the company I represent, I should immediately launch into my sales presentation?" This may or may not be required; much will depend on your judgment in sizing up prospects and the background of the situation. Experienced sales professionals recognize that, in their daily activities, prospects and customers can be categorized according to their particular type of buying problems. The categories are:

✓ Regular customers whose attention can be readily secured because they have had a series of previous experiences with the sales professional.

✓ New contacts who recognize a need for the product and whose desire for that particular class of goods is already stimulated. The primary emphasis here is to show them that your product or service is the one best solution among all competitors.

✓ Contacts who recognize the problem and a generic solution. The task here is to make these willing buyers *prefer* your product.

✓ Prospects who recognize neither the problem nor the solution. They're satisfied with things as they are and do not evidence any need. The task here is to make them recognize both.

Keep in mind that the attention stage is actually divided into two parts: (1) the preliminary social aspects—the amenities, which vary in the time that should be devoted to them; and (2) the focusing of the prospect's attention on your product or service. The transition from self to product must, in all cases, be a smooth one. Witness the following illustration:

PROSPECT: [speaking at some length about a problem with one of the company's older calculators] ". . . and what a time they had trying to come up with the figures on this deal—three people were checking the figures, or at least trying to, and . . . . "

SALES PROFESSIONAL: [moving in at the proper moment; in this case, the prospect had taken a deep breath before continuing] "I'll bet you were wondering just when you would get an accurate figure. That's why you'll be pleased with the speed and the accuracy of this miniature transistorized calculator that not only will do the work quickly, but also . . . [the sales professional then continues the presentation]."

In the preliminary social aspects, you must exhibit attention and an understanding of the amenities and the prospect's problems before you can proceed with the actual purpose of your

call. There will be many times when the amenities must be min-
imized and you will need to get to your point at once. When that
happens, engage in only a very brief exchange of greetings, and
quickly get settled. In all situations, use your judgment and take
your cue from prospects. Watch their faces and gestures, and
be alert to their tone of voice; they give powerful and constant
communications.

## How to Secure Attention

Having accomplished the preliminary social aspects, you can
now direct the prospect's attention to your product or service.
Now is the time to open your sales presentation with a direct
statement based on the benefits to be derived from the ownership
or use of your product or service. Make these opening statements
so effective that prospects will give their undivided attention to
your presentation.

Familiarize yourself with the seven techniques that follow.
Become proficient in their use—most especially, those with
which you feel at ease. Direct every word to the plans, ambitions,
and problems of your listener. Only then can your presentation
be effective.

### 1.  *Focus immediately on a benefit.*

Right at the start, show prospects how they will benefit from
your proposition. Make your statements powerful, so that the average individual would have to be unreasonable not to listen to
your presentation. The skill lies in addressing prospects so that,
as reasonable people, they won't be able to say no at this point,
and you can describe your product's further advantages. Some
examples:

> ✓ "I want to show you how to reduce your packaging costs
> by [dollar amount] per day."

✓ "This gravity feed system will eliminate three extra handlings of this material; two workers will be able to do the present work of three."

With statements such as these, the sales professional has reached over into the interest stage. Prospects have been told immediately what they will derive from the use of the products.

### 2. Start with a question.

Questions are a quick means for gaining the attention of a prospect. They can be used frequently as "openers." Just plan them carefully, to ensure their simplicity, directness, and tact. Avoid assiduously the hackneyed and foolish ones, such as "What's new?" or "Anything I can interest you in while I'm here?" How much better to use the questions that follow:

✓ "Tell me, would you be in business tomorrow if your business records were destroyed by fire tonight?"

✓ "Did you ever stop to think that not everyone can get insurance?"

### 3. Begin with an unusual or shocking opener.

An unusual or shocking opener arouses curiosity and provides an excellent opportunity for showmanship. Directed to your offering, it can be a most effective beginning. Insurance sales professionals certainly win their prospects' attention when they take a sample home mortgage from their briefcase and tear it up, saying, "You can do this, too!" A sales professional for a fountain pen manufacturer—whose products, it was claimed, would not leak—used an unusual and shocking technique to command the immediate attention of his prospects. He would take out a bottle of ink, fill his pen, and then violently shake it up and down toward his clothing. As he performed this action, he would say, "It won't leak because it can't leak!"

### 4.  Relate an interesting, sales-related anecdote.

Consider narrating interesting, sales-connected anecdotes. These can be brief accounts of pertinent incidents and examples, or true stories of special significance to prospects and the problems they face. Deliver your anecdotes skillfully. Practice building up a suspense that compels attention and makes the prospect eager to know the outcome. The examples that follow illustrate the point.

SALES PROFESSIONAL: [sells mutual funds for investment purposes]: "Experience may be a great teacher, [Prospect's Name], but it's frequently an expensive one. A good customer brought this home forcefully only this past week. This was the story he related to me: 'Some years ago, our family lost everything—we invested our entire savings in things we knew nothing about. Seems impossible that *we* could have done that without any advice—we're a family that would permit only an expert to make even a minor house repair.' That experience, [Prospect's Name], has been an object lesson, and my client was determined that his newly accumulated nest egg would be invested more wisely. Yes, he wanted a return on his money, but there was something more he had to be assured of: expert advice that would mean security and peace of mind. He recognized that no one individual can employ a corps of experts for himself. That is why he entrusted his precious savings to a mutual fund. He knew that the finest financial experts would be directing their undivided attention to his interests and those of others who invest in the fund."

Just make certain that your anecdote is a true story and is related to the experiences of others whom you have satisfied with your product. Develop a facility to heighten suspense as you relate a story. Note the technique in the following narrative:

SALES PROFESSIONAL [sells fire extinguishers for industrial use]: "You can learn from what happens to you, but what a price some companies have to pay learning it. I just heard from a plant manager this past week—and a happy manager he is. He took what we believe to be some excellent advice. This is what he told me. It seems that a maintenance manager in another plant had an absolute "No" for anybody who suggested the new, more modern type of fire extinguishers. He felt that the sprinkling system that covered most of the building was more than adequate, and there were fire hoses in various locations. Nothing could happen to them. Well, it did. A fire started in a room not covered by the sprinkler system and not readily accessible to the use of a hose. The small fire that started could readily have been controlled with a modern fire extinguisher. But, of course, they didn't have any. The insurance covered the financial loss, but the plant operation was interrupted for five days."

### 5. Use familiar and important names.

Recognizable and impressive names—either of local or national importance to the prospect or customer—can command the prospect's positive and respectful attention.

### 6. Open with an exhibit.

In some cases, it may be wise to begin with an exhibit. Some products and services lend themselves especially to this technique. In using this opener, the sales professional makes the product or related material—component parts, portfolios, photographs, or models—the focus of attention.

### 7. Try news and sales suggestions.

There are sales professionals who prefer to use, whenever possible, news items as selling suggestions. These are always appropriate and useful for sales professionals who call regularly on the same accounts. They tell their prospects and customers about what is happening in their line of business and in related industries. They try to always lace such information with practical suggestions that contribute to increased sales. Trade papers, financial papers, and other related business publications will supply many items of general interest. Selling suggestions—for example, how to improve window, counter, and other interior and exterior displays, or how new and more efficient uses for advertising materials and sales promotion ideas can increase profits—will be of real interest. Don't just say that you think a new display or a piece of advertising copy is a good idea. To impress them and command their undivided attention, you might tell them:

SALES PROFESSIONAL: "This type of display, changed once a week, produced a 15 percent traffic increase for [Name Company]."

## Additional Considerations to Observe

*Try to avoid discussions on subjects that are controversial and that tend to stimulate deeply rooted, intense personal feelings. Avoid, whenever possible, discussions on political, social, and religious themes; there are other more interesting and agreeable topics that can make a much better contribution to the interview situation.*

Sales professionals may wonder what to do when third parties are on the scene when they call, or how to avoid interruptions that challenge their ability to hold the listener's attention. Here is what to do in these instances.

If a third party or a number of interested persons are present—for example, in negotiations for equipment that requires multiple buying decisions—make it a point to direct your talk to everyone present. You will usually find that one individual in the group is the dominant personality. When you know who this is, direct your strongest attention to him or her. If you can avoid it, don't give your sales presentation when a competitor is present; use every effort to avoid this situation. When faced with interruptions—assistants who break in on your discussion from time to time; a telephone that rings too often; routine demands on prospects that compromise their ability to focus attention on your proposition—do the following. After each interruption, refocus the prospect's attention as quickly as possible by repeating the statement you made immediately preceding the interruption. Explain gently to the prospect why his or her uninterrupted attention will be repaid in the value of your product. As a last resort, you can tactfully ask for another appointment at a time when the discussions can be more advantageously pursued.

## Your Final Objective

Having secured the undivided attention of the prospect, you should now make every effort to heighten his or her interest. This is the second stage in the prospect's mental buying process—*the interest stage.* Now is the time for attention to the benefits and advantages of your offering to be expanded and developed. Keep in mind that in these first two stages—attention and interest—and in the remaining stages, no boundary line separates one from the other. The steps are discussed separately here only for purposes of analysis; in an actual sales situation, these various stages will blend smoothly one into the other. An easy transition from one stage to the next provides an even-flowing movement toward the ultimate goal—the final closing of the sale. In the actual business of selling, the securing of the prospect's attention and the heightening of his or her interest are usually so interrelated and overlapped that, in retrospect, you will find it difficult to detect precisely when and where "attention" left off and "interest" began.

## Make Prospects Want to Hear More

Through your enthusiasm and genuine pride in your offering, you should further impress your prospects with your confidence in the worth of your proposition for them. They should want to hear more about your products or services because their attention has been activated. Their interest has developed into a definite sense of concern for themselves personally, for their business, or for both. This concern is accomplished by supplying them with a few specific—not general—selling points that indicate how your product or service will better serve their particular interests. At this stage, you will not present them with the total picture. Rather, you will whet their appetites; they will want to hear more. When this has been accomplished, you are in a position to move to the heart of your presentation.

Be sure to develop the interest stage carefully; structure your sales presentation in terms of the prospect's self-interest. Remember, people do not purchase goods or services; they purchase the benefits and advantages that these various goods and services can provide. Learn quickly to concentrate on the prospect's point of view.

## The Art of Listening

The art of directed listening was touched on in Chapter 1. It is appropriate, however, to emphasize again that you must tune in to the customer's viewpoint. You can do this only by directed listening. Ask questions that stimulate prospects to talk about their problems, and always give them an uninterrupted opportunity to express themselves when they answer. Don't rush to fill the gap if there is a brief pause while they consider their answers. Give them time—the "pros" always do! In this early stage, avoid talking too much. Listen carefully; you will then be able to supply some specific facts at an earlier moment in the interview. Prospects' sales talk, particularly in these early stages of attention and interest, provides you with their dominant and related motivations for wanting your product or service. Effective directed listening will enable you to take mental note of *what the customer is buying* or wants to buy, rather than what you are trying to sell. Armed with this information, you will find the selling task considerably easier.

You should now be in a position to move into the core of the interview. Prospects should have been moved to a point in the buying process where their desire for your product or service is heightened. You are ready to convince them, with a sound presentation, that your products or services can best satisfy their needs and can solve their problems more effectively than anything else available to them.

## Selling by the Rules

Close your eyes for a moment, uncross your legs, and link your hands across your lap. This is not so you can have a quick catnap. Instead, this exercise is useful for you to use your own experience to realize you need to be perceived as a consultant, not a salesperson, and that prospects must trust you before they will buy from you.

With your eyes closed, focus on the most recent significant purchase you made. Was it a camera? A car? A boat? A hi-fi system? Or something more necessary but less glamorous?

How did you go about buying it? Did you do any research beforehand? Did you have any preconceived ideas of what you wanted? What helped you make your decision? Was the sales professional who sold it to you persuasive? Did you end up with something you didn't originally plan for? If this didn't happen at this recent purchase, has it ever happened to you? If so, what was it that turned you around?

OK, now open your eyes. In fact, open your eyes in more than one sense.

How often have you bought something you did not want? You started off wanting something, and you had a fixed budget in mind. But you came home from the store after spending far more than the figure you had budgeted. The truth of what we have spent only comes home when the bill comes through the door.

Take, for example, the story of a middle-aged woman who needed a new vacuum cleaner. She didn't want to buy one, but she knew she needed one. So she decided to spend as little as possible on a new vacuum cleaner and grudgingly went to buy the best of the cheapest. A bright and energetic sales professional spotted her and immediately assumed, wrongly, that she was happy about the impending purchase. You might be reading this and thinking, "What has this got to do with the products and services I sell?" Well, it has everything to do with your line of business. Are you the bright sales professional spotting someone with a need? It is your job, your passion, your life. But are you under the misconception that your prospects should be as excited as you are about your profession? They are not. How can they be turned around?

Let's get back to the vacuum cleaner story. "You want a vacuum cleaner?" the sales professional said. "No," she replied, "I *need* one." The sales professional countered, "I see you are looking at our Hoover Super Light economy model. This is one that people like to use—especially older people—because it's cheap and light to push around."

She looked down at it and pushed it aside, thinking to herself, "I'm still trim and in the prime of my life—I'm not yet ready for the Hoover Super Light vintage." The sales professional then asked the "got-you" question—a question that can only be answered in favor of the salesperson, whether the prospect's reply is positive or negative: "Do you have children or pets?"

Think of how many people have children and/or pets. Then add on those who cannot distinguish between the two. Any sales professional has a 99.9 percent chance of hearing the right answer and being able to pursue the sale with no "get-out" clause.

Because the sales professional asked that question, the woman's mind turned from vacuum cleaners to her two cats. Her cats, she said, are her pride and joy; they make her feel "so special." "And yes," she told him, "one has got long hair; it's a Persian." That was all he needed. She had given away the whole truth. She had to have the best vacuum cleaner because there were cat hairs everywhere in her house, and only the very, *very* best vacuum cleaner will suck them all up.

Ultimately, she bought the best, most expensive model, far above her budget. But she still felt smug about spotting all the selling signals given by the sales professional and not having been taken in by them. In fact, as she walked to her car, alongside the sales professional, who was carrying the newly purchased vacuum cleaner, she complimented him on his sales ability. "Oh no," he said, as if insulted. "I don't *sell* at all. We have strict regular meetings with our manager every three months. We have to learn everything about the new products and then, when customers come into the store, I ask them questions just to identify what will really suit their needs. I take great pride in knowing all I can about the products and then satisfying those needs. The pride comes in finding the right tool to do the right job for the right customer."

Is this where *your* strengths lie? Do you learn all you can about your products and then use your skills to match the prospect's needs to the appropriate product?

Some customers buy for the wrong reasons and then suffer "buyer's remorse." What they bought isn't what they thought it was, and you have to take it back. Do sales professionals suffer remorse because of bad selling, or because of unprepared buying, or because the product does not stand up to its presale description?

What is it that makes prospects want to buy? More importantly, what makes prospects *not* want to buy—even when they may really need something? No one likes the thought of being sold to. People like to think they buy something because it's their choice. They are too smart to be forced into a purchase. They are intelligent and frugal enough to know what they want and what they can afford. No smart sales professional is going to persuade them any other way.

If this is the way you think about your purchases, what would make your clients any different? You will hear or read about hundreds of sales ideas, but if these are used out of context and not as part of a process, they will not work.

So, the first rule of a successful selling process is: *Make sure you are not perceived as selling anything.* People want to buy, they do not want to be sold to. Think about this. Is this true of you? Is it true of your customers? How then, as a sales professional, do you apply this rule?

When asked what you do for a living, do you often avoid the word "sales" and create little puzzle-like clues as to what you do? For example, someone in the financial services industry might say, "I create dreams and help avoid nightmares." What sort of title do you give yourself? How do you wish to be perceived? If you apply the first rule of not being perceived as selling anything, you then must apply the second rule: *Before prospects buy from you, they have to trust you.* Prospects have to trust that you want the best for them, trust your knowledge, and trust your word. How do you acquire trust? Are there any sessions on building trust? We know the depth and meaning of the word in legal terms and we acknowledge how binding and honest trust must be, but what is being referred to is an intangible trust—something that grows and develops when nurtured.

It is difficult to build trust from a standing start. Cold calling is a good example. Many sales professionals have had to start this way, and their first sales probably resulted, unknowingly, from some obscure reason, such as:

✓ "You drive the same car as my dad. You must be a person of integrity. Yes, I trust what you say. I will buy from you."

✓ "My father bought the same product from the same company as yours. He bought it for us when we were kids. I would like to do the same for my family. Yes, I trust you."

Or, conversely:

✓ "My ex-husband placed all his business with your company. I wouldn't dream of placing any business with you." [This implies, "I don't trust him, I don't trust you."]

Trust comes from a number of sources. Sometimes, it is built on a quality that has nothing to do with your business advice but is linked to your being an adviser who does the little extra things. One MDRT sales professional said it best in this example.

"I know a client, a delightful little old lady who was referred to me by an attorney. She was very suspicious of anyone new and only agreed to see me because I had been referred by her attorney. My meeting with her was going to be on a three-way basis. The attorney could introduce me and if he agreed with what I said, then so would she. We agreed to meet at her home at an appointed time.

"She lived by herself and was suspicious of people whom she did not know. I telephoned her home to say I was on my way, and I telephoned again when I arrived. She told me the attorney had not yet arrived, but she was prepared to meet me first. It was because I had spoken to her a few times previously, and put her at her ease, she was prepared to see me alone. By the time the attorney had arrived, he was totally unnecessary for the meeting, but he had been needed to confirm the *initial* trust in me."

The sales professional continued: "The next time I met my client, I was aware that she was concerned about something. She had been awaiting a security telephone that could be activated should she be taken ill. Social Services had agreed to get back to her but had not. I called them immediately, whilst at her home, and got the security phone installed in the afternoon. From this moment on, my client had complete trust in my advice because I had spotted the real thing that was bothering her. She now has faith in my ability to look after her wants and needs. Because of this 'extra' help, it was as if my investment advice was almost superfluous. These were my main reasons for being there, but not her priority at the time."

This level of advice and care is a great responsibility, but it is also a tremendous honor to know someone has such trust in you. It is also a great insight and a confirmation that the strangest reasons can result in trust, and the most insignificant things can take trust away. Loyalty creates future business and great job satisfaction.

To create trust, two things are important: how you are seen and perceived in a particular time frame, and whether your prospect is having a good or bad day or a good or bad experience. Never take all the blame or all the praise. Instead, learn the third rule of successful selling: *Find the warm button and press it.* What is important, at that very moment, to your prospect or customer? Don't just ask. Find out by listening. Pickup what appear to be insignificant throwaway words, and explore them.

Here's another example from an MDRT sales professional.

"I had a client who came to talk about pensions. Now, everyone is different. Some people who want a pension just want to set it up and leave, while others want to know the specific details. I must always listen and pick up points and see if my clients wish for me to develop them. This client, who came to talk about pensions, walked in, shook my hand, and said, 'Hello, it's a lovely day for wind surfing, isn't it?' Unless I'm perceptive, I might not actually hear any of this. All that is heard is a little voice in my head saying, 'Here he is, on time, and he is going to purchase a pension plan.' The client then sat down. Forms were retrieved, and quotations then presented, to which he says, 'Oh, when this money matures on retirement, I will be able to buy a really big van to take out wind surfing.' Again, unless I'm perceptive, I don't hear this. I need to talk about retirement planning—how much to put in, how much will it pay out—so I ask about his current occupation and income. 'Yes, my work gives me plenty of time off so I can go wind surfing.' By this time, the penny has dropped. He actually wants me to say, 'Are you interested in wind surfing?' To which the floodgates open. 'Yes, I'm Welsh champion. I didn't start doing this until I was in my late forties, and now I spend all weekends wind surfing and I am very proud of my achievements.' But his inner voice is saying to him, 'This salesperson is really interested in me and what I do, what I want to achieve. I am glad I have an adviser like this who really understands me and my wants.' To him, what I sell is necessary but not a priority. As a sales professional, however, I also need to recognize the pride that he feels and, therefore, have an interest in his well-being, which is as important as my investment advice. My advice to him became a subsidiary to his real interest."

What does this mean? You must learn to speak your prospects' language. Even though they come to you at times to observe your products and services, they really want to know if you understand them. They will rely on your knowledge of your products and your expertise in supplying their wants and needs, if you exhibit a feeling for them as people.

The concept of cold calling has already been mentioned. A referral is very much a warm lead, so setting up a meeting will probably not be an issue. In fact, the prospect will probably say, "Oh yes, I'm glad you called. I need someone to tell me about this product I'm interested in. [Referrer's Name] said you would be getting in touch with me."

Your first job is to prove the trust the referral has conveyed. A referred prospect will almost always report back to the referrer, especially if a professional introduction is involved. If accountants or attorneys refer someone to you, they are putting their own reputation at stake. Unless they are completely happy with your services, they will be very uncomfortable about referring people to you. Conversely, if they refer someone who is then very happy with your services, their good judgment and their worth as advisers gain extra affirmation.

Here is another MDRT case in point.

"I was referred to a client by a local accountant. The prospect had other advisers before, but was not entirely happy with their advice." (Often, when you are told this, you might assume that the earlier advisers did not know their stuff. But is this strictly true? Instead, did they fail to get to know their clients? Were they then perceived as bad advisers and therefore couldn't sell the product?)

"I had a meeting with the prospect, who gave me details of his current portfolio and his plans to amend it to adapt to changing circumstances. He asked a lot of technical questions, the ones that make you think, 'He's not asking these because he wants an answer; he is asking these because he wants to test my knowledge.' So I either had to try to answer with the correct technical data or say, 'This point is interesting. Why did you ask it?' Answering this way results in the prospect's self-answering the query (to show how knowledgeable he or she is), or asking in a different way and giving you more of a guide as to what the question really is.

"During my meeting with this prospect, we started talking about what I did prior to working in my business. I explained I had been a teacher specializing in the environment and art, and that, while teaching, I had an interest in the ginkgo tree. Why I mentioned this I have no idea, but suddenly my prospect's attitude changed completely. He beamed, 'You know the ginkgo?' We then had a fascinating conversation on the merits and history of the ginkgo.

"The ginkgo is the most primitive form of tree that has sustained its primitive form throughout centuries. It is used extensively for medical research. My prospect, a pharmacist, had just completed a detailed research project on the ginkgo tree. So, immediately, he saw me as someone with knowledge, understanding, and a complete empathy for something that was very important to him. My advice was immediately put above all other advisers.' And he has become one of my greatest and closest clients with whom there is a great deal of mutual respect, rapport, and understanding, simply as a result of the insignificant ginkgo tree."

True, there is a fine line between good conversations that can lead nowhere and conversations that can hinder you in getting down to the priority of selling. Yet, if there is an opportunity to pick up on something that has real significance to a prospect, this interchange can develop a new depth in your relationship. You don't need a hard sell because you have a harmonious understanding of your prospect's needs.

This leads to two key components of selling: honesty and integrity. You must, however, let sincerity follow, and do what you promise. If you cannot deliver the goods when things go wrong, then you must communicate and come clean that you have made a mistake.

At work, you need to be a person of integrity—someone who doesn't take shortcuts. If something goes wrong or things do not happen as you thought they might, then you must stand tall and face the situation. An admission of a mistake leads to immeasurable trust and, in the end, reaps greater harvests. One wrong move, perhaps because of fear of what might happen, will destroy your reputation forever. Just as trust can be built on some very obscure reason, the loss of trust and sincerity can come from a similarly obscure source.

## Building Up a Supportive Team

Sincerity and trust must also be the hallmarks of your support staff, if you have any. Having people you can trust will preserve your own sanity and ease the administrative load connected to your work. It is not worth your while to build up a healthy rapport with your clients, only to lose it or have to repair it because of administrative errors. They can lead to mistrust, even though the fault is not directly yours.

As an example, imagine a person who owns a Jaguar, which contains a world-class motor. During a service call, by mistake, water is placed in the fuel tank. The car's performance greatly diminishes and the frustrated owner blames the vehicle's design and engineering. He eventually sells the car and says he will never buy another Jaguar. The car lost its credibility with that owner, even though the problem had nothing to do with the car at all.

Another example has been experienced by many people. You go to a local restaurant and you are greeted by a less-than-cordial server. You can see the server's badge; on it is written: "Happy to be of service." But you soon realize that the badge should have carried a health warning. You say, "Excuse me, I wonder if . . . ," but you are cut short by a gruff query: "What do you want?"

It's strange, isn't it? As good as the restaurant's food is, your probably won't go back there again. The server has left a bad memory, a poor impression. Does this happen when your clients ring in? What sort of reception or impression is your support staff giving? Do you know? Perhaps you should find out from your clients how they are received when they try to contact you, and how they perceive this reception.

## You've Sold It; Don't Buy It Back

How often have you prepared for a really important sales presentation? Because your presentation is everything, you've researched your products, anticipated closing problems, supplied enough visuals and graphs to impress even Disney, and mouthed power phrases first thing in the morning, in front of a mirror.

You arrive early, you wait in anticipation, mentally practicing your presentation, and then you are shown in. After initial pleasantries, you take a deep breath and begin. You're at a stage where you have to be extra wary—not of the prospect, but of yourself! You've prepared your talk, and nobody is going to stop you.

Part way through your opening paragraph, the prospect gives you a buying signal that you recognize but ignore. Why? Because you *prepared,* and nobody is going to stop you! Just remember, however much you have prepared a presentation, be equally prepared to adapt it. If you sell something early, don't buy it back!

## How to Use Personal Dynamics for More Productive Selling

In your dealings with prospects, have you ever had a personality conflict while attempting a sale? All sales professionals, at one time or another, have experienced not being able to get on the same wavelength as their prospects.

You have probably had the opposite experience as well. You meet prospects, and within the first ten or fifteen minutes, you feel as if you have known them for ten or fifteen years. Has that response of immediate chemistry ever happened to you?

Creating an instant rapport with prospects can be accomplished by honoring selling's Golden Rule: *Learn how to do what prospects want done.* You can create a lot more chemistry and a lot less conflict, depending on how well you practice the

Golden Rule. If you practice it appropriately, there will be more chemistry and less conflict. If you take the opposite approach and practice it inappropriately, the result will be more conflict and less chemistry.

The biblical Golden Rule is: "Do unto others as you would have them do unto you." If you are a manager, it means managing people the way you would like to be managed. If you are a sales professional, it means selling to people in the way you would like to be treated as a buyer. In reality, you need to practice the spirit and intent of another rule—let's call it the Platinum Rule: "Do unto others the way they want to be done unto." Treat people the way they want to be treated.

There are various ways to size up prospects and get on their wavelength. These are the early steps in positively influencing their ideas, their attitudes, their opinions, and, most importantly, their buying behavior. Have you been exposed to the concept that people can be profiled as having particular personality styles by observing two simple aspects of their behavior: *openness* and *directness?*

Everyone uses some level of openness and directness in communicating with people. Your level of openness and directness forms your personality style. When you identify your personality pattern and understand what your prospects' patterns are, you will know what needs to be done differently to get on their wavelength and make them feel more comfortable with you, your products, and your services.

Openness is defined as the readiness and willingness of people to outwardly show and share their feelings and thoughts. Directness is how people pace themselves and the way they view risk, change, and decision making. Let's find out how open you are by describing self-contained behaviors and open behaviors and letting you determine which description best fits you. Think about the people you work with, live with, and do business with. What are their levels of openness?

Self-contained people do not show or share their feelings and thoughts very readily. In fact, they are often described as having "a poker face," being hard to read, and not showing much body language. Most times, they hold their cards close to their vests, and they don't like to get close physically or mentally. They are not "contact people." In fact, when they meet others for the very first time, they stand farther away. In selling, they are the prospects who, when they speak to you, tend to organize their thoughts before delivering them. When you get off the subject, they say things like, "Well, where's all this leading? I'm not quite sure I'm following. What's the bottom line?" When it comes to decision making, they depend on logic, facts, details, and proof. To them, time is money. How many of your prospects fit this description?

Open people are very animated. When you tell them something upsetting, they show distress. When you tell them something exciting, they get excited. You can read them like a book; they wear their hearts on their sleeves. Open people get close physically and mentally. They greet others with hugs and kisses, and they will often take advantage of a promising situation. They're physical people.

In a selling scenario, they have a tendency to get off the subject when talking to you. "That reminds me of . . ." or "You think that's good, wait until you hear this one," and pretty soon they forget what you were talking about. When you have spent time with someone who is very open and you walk away from the conversation, you tend to say, "Wow, what did we talk about? But it was exciting, I'll tell you that!" When personal buying decisions must be made, this type of prospect is guided by emotions, gut feelings, and intuition. Regarding time, the attitude is: "I may come early, I may come late, I may never show up at all."

Where do you see yourself on the openness scale? Pick a number from 1 to 4, with 1 being the most self-contained and 4 being the most open. Hold on to that number; we'll be coming back to it.

Now let's determine how direct you are. Indirect people tend to come across as more guarded. They are more introverted and are averse to risk. They approach risks, decisions, and change slowly and cautiously because they do not want to be wrong. They mull things over; they listen more, and they ask a lot more questions. In selling situations, these prospects are input-oriented and want to gather more information about products and services because they don't want to make a buying mistake. The bottom line: They move a bit slower. Direct people, on the other hand, move at a faster pace. When they face risk, decisions, or change, they approach surely and quickly. They care less about quality than about quantity—less about failures than about successes. What's the best way to get successes? Do as much as possible.

Indirect people go for quality rather than quantity. Indirect people follow the rules. If they shouldn't do something, they won't. If the rule says, "You should," they will. When there's a gray area, where the rules aren't clearly stated and policies and procedures haven't been spelled out, they will not do something without asking permission. Direct people handle gray areas very differently. If the rules say they shouldn't do something, they might go ahead anyway. Their attitude is that rules are made to be broken. To them, a rule is only a guideline. When they approach a gray area where rules aren't clearly spelled out, they say "Bingo!" They call it their "window of opportunity." Their attitude toward gray areas is: "It's easier to beg forgiveness than to seek permission."

Now it's time to determine your personality type. First, let's determine how direct you are. Using a scale from A to D, with A being the most direct and D being the least direct, choose one letter. What does this all mean? Go back to how you graded your openness, and then find your personality type on this chart:

| Level of Openness | Level of Directness | Personality Type |
|---|---|---|
| 1 or 2 | A or B | Thinker |
| 1 or 2 | C or D | Director |
| 3 or 4 | A or B | Relater |
| 3 or 4 | C or D | Socializer |

This model identifies people as having four core behavioral styles. Although most people can identify with some aspects of each style, there does seem to be a *primary* style that each person uses.

The key to this concept of four personality styles is not just understanding your style, but understanding the styles of your prospects and clients. If you understand their styles, you can then start thinking in their language—doing things that make them comfortable with you. You can do several things to be more flexible in your interactions with each of the four basic styles.

## Thinkers: Traits

Thinkers are detail-oriented, analytical, persistent, and systematic problem solvers. They are more concerned with content than style. Thinkers prefer involvement with products and services under specific, and preferably controlled, conditions so that performance, process, and results can be perfected.

Thinkers are uncomfortable with emotionality and irrationality in others, and they strive to avoid embarrassment by attempting to control both their actions and their emotions. Thinkers like to operate at a steady pace that allows them to check and recheck their work. They tend to see the serious, more complicated sides of situations, but their natural mental wit often allows them to appreciate the lighter side of things.

Thinkers demand a lot from themselves and others, and they may succumb to overly critical tendencies. They typically share information, positive or negative, only on a need-to-know basis. When thinkers have definite knowledge of facts and details, they quietly hold their ground. Their strengths include accuracy, dependability, independence, clarification and testing skills, follow-through, and organization.

Thinkers often become irritated by surprises and glitches. They tend to be skeptical, and they like to see things in writing. Because thinkers need to be right, they prefer checking processes themselves. This tendency toward perfectionism, taken to an extreme, can result in "paralysis by overanalysis." After determining the specific risks, margins of error, and other variables that significantly influence the desired results, they will take action.

Thinkers can be seen as aloof, picky, and critical. Although thinkers are good listeners and ask a lot of questions, they often focus too much on details and miss the big picture. Professions that use thinkers' analytical skills and tendency toward perfection are ideal. Thinkers are often engineers, statisticians, computer programmers, and surgeons.

## Interacting with Thinkers

Because thinkers have the most complex thought patterns, they base their decisions on proven information and track records. They want to make rational choices based on facts, not on other people's opinions or testimonials. In a sales situation, when thinkers say, "I need to think about it," they usually mean it. You can help them make a decision by supplying the materials they request and by allowing them the time to make the right decision for themselves. Focus on emphasizing deadlines so that thinkers can build those time frames into their procedures.

When you're coaching thinkers, demonstrate a procedure in an efficient, logical manner, stressing the purpose of each step.

Continue at a relatively slower pace, and stop at each key place in the process to make sure you're being understood. Ask for possible input. This approach ensures success with the task and minimization of stress for thinkers.

If you want to motivate thinkers, appeal to their need for accuracy and logic. This personality type doesn't respond well to fancy verbal antics, so keep your approach clear, clean, and documentable. Better yet, provide illustration and documentation. Avoid exaggeration and vagueness. Show them how yours is the best available current option.

The best way to correct thinkers is to show them the way to get a job done. Typically, they'll master the format, then modify it to suit their individual needs. They tend to start with what they have to work with, but will then personalize it, almost from the beginning, so that it works better as they see it. In this way, they can often avoid people who, they perceive, might tell them to do things differently. This is one way thinkers maintain control of their work. They tend to sidestep authorities who they think are endeavoring to correct them. At the extreme, this behavior can appear sneaky to other types, especially if the thinkers get caught.

Specify the exact behavior that is indicated, and outline how you would like to see it changed. Establish agreed-on checkpoints and times. Allow thinkers to save face. Remember how much they fear being wrong. While you're communicating with thinkers, be well organized and clear in your statements. They are likely to ask lots of questions about a situation or subject, in their search for a logical conclusion. You may want to have them clarify their more pressing key concerns.

It isn't always easy to acknowledge the achievements of thinkers. Focus on how much you appreciate the high personal standards they set for themselves. Cite a specific and appropriate example that proves this point. Then, notice their reaction. If they show discomfort, tell them that you did not mean to embarrass them, but only intended to let them know how much you value them. If their reactions are more positive, ask them to tell you more about the sense of satisfaction and enjoyment they derive from similar things.

Before delegating a task to thinkers, take time to answer their most critical questions about the structure and/or the guidance they require in a specific situation. The more they understand the details, the more likely they will complete the task properly. Be sure to establish deadlines.

Are you a thinker? If you are, here are some tips to make it easier to relate to the other three personality types. Modify your criticism, spoken or unspoken, of others' work. Check things less often—or only check the critical things as opposed to checking everything. This will allow the flow of a process to continue. Ease up on controlling your emotions. Try to engage in more water-cooler interaction. Accept the fact that you can have high standards without expecting perfection of yourself or others. Occasionally confront colleagues (or a boss) with whom you disagree, instead of avoiding or ignoring them and then doing what you want to do anyway. Tone down the tendency to overprepare. A little spontaneity can add spice to your approach in sales.

## Directors: Traits

Directors are driven by an inner need to lead and be in personal control. They want to take charge of people and situations so they can reach their goals. Their key need is achieving, so they seek no-nonsense, bottom-line results. Their motto is: "Lead, follow, or get out of the way." Directors want to win, so they often challenge people or rules. They accept challenges, take authority, and plunge headfirst into solving problems. They tend to exhibit great administrative and operational skills, and they work quickly and impressively by themselves.

Directors have the ability to focus on one task, to the exclusion of everything else. They can block out doorbells, sirens, or other people, and channel all their energies into the specific job at hand. Their complete focus on their own goals and the task at hand can make them appear aloof and cool. Directors can be so single-minded that they forget to take the time to "smell the roses." And if they do remember, they may return and comment, "I smelled 12 roses today . . . how many did you smell?"

Closely allied to their positive traits are the negative traits of stubbornness, impatience, and toughness. Directors tend to take control of other people and often have a low tolerance for feelings, attitudes, and inadequacies of coworkers and subordinates.

Directors like to move at a fast pace and are impatient with delays. It is not unusual for directors to call and launch into a conversation without saying, "Hello." Directors are often found in top management, but their skills also make them ideal as hard-driving reporters, stockbrokers, independent consultants, or drill sergeants! Under pressure, they often get rid of their anger by ranting, raving, or challenging others. Their ways of relieving their own inner tensions often create stress and tension in others.

## Interacting with Directors

With directors, you can agree on the goal and specify the boundaries of the playing field, but then get out of their way. Remember, directors like to learn the basic steps for quickly sifting out what they want. In the interest of saving time, directors may try to find shortcuts, so show them the simplest and fastest route to their stated destination. To motivate directors, you should provide them with options and clearly describe the probabilities of success. When you want to flatter directors, mention their achievements and leadership potential. Omit personal comments, and focus on their track record.

When you're communicating with them, be prepared to listen to their suggestions, the course of action they have in mind, and the general results they're considering. This will help you begin on a positive note by highlighting the initial areas of agreement.

If you want to give advice to directors—and get them to take it—stick to the facts. Draw them out by talking about the desired results. Then discuss their concerns. Focus on tasks more than feelings. Ask them how *they* would solve a problem. To correct directors, or get them to alter their course, describe the results that are desired. Show them the gap between actual and desired results. Suggest the improvement that's needed, then establish a time when they're to get back to you.

If you delegate tasks to directors, give them the bottom line and then let them "do their thing." Give them parameters, guidelines, and deadlines so they can be more efficient. If you're a director, you run the risk of turning people off—not on purpose, but because your actions are so strong and direct. Here are some techniques for being more successful:

✓ Allow others to do things without excessive or untimely interference. Make assignments, set deadlines, and then leave your people alone!

✓ When you're participating in a group, resist the expectation to always be in charge. You might have to consciously remind yourself to be second-chair, but it will be worth it in terms of staff development and idea exchange.

✓ Modify your tendency to give *orders* to others. Try to change them into requests or suggestions whenever possible.

✓ Enlist the support of others, and get their input. Make joint projects truly joint projects, even if it means sitting down ahead of time and listing your specific duties in the projects. Give others credit when their accomplishments deserve it.

✓ Praise people for jobs well done, and let people know that it's only natural to have mistakes happen.

✓ When you're delegating, give some *authority* along with the responsibility.

## Relaters: Traits

Relaters are warm, supportive, and reliable. They are the most people-oriented of all of the four styles. Relaters are excellent listeners. They develop strong networks of people who are willing to be mutually supportive. Relaters are irritated by pushy, aggressive behavior. They are cooperative and steady workers, and excellent team players. "Risk" is an ugly word to relaters. They may even stay in an unpleasant environment rather than risk a change. Disruption in their routines can cause them distress. If they are faced with a change, they need to think it through carefully and plan for it.

Relaters yearn for more tranquillity and security in their lives than the other three types do. They have a natural need for composure, stability, and balance. Their relaxed disposition makes them approachable and warm. They are courteous, friendly, and willing to share responsibilities. They are also good planners who persist and generally follow through with their plans.

Relaters appear to go along with others even when they inwardly do not agree. This tendency creates an environment in which more aggressive types may take advantage of the relaters. Their lack of assertiveness sometimes results in hurt feelings because they do not let others know how they truly feel. They can be overly sensitive and easily bullied.

Their need for security makes them very slow at making decisions. This slowness results from their need to avoid risk and unknown situations, and their desire to include others in the decision-making process.

Relaters are often found in the helping professions, such as counseling, teaching, social work, the ministry, psychology, nursing, and human resource development. Relaters make the most patient and supportive parents.

## Interacting with Relaters

Relaters contribute stability and perseverance to their workplace. Because they work toward harmony in the office, they usually fit comfortably into the work environment, but they may become used to repeating the same old methods again and again. They may improve their work practices by utilizing shortcuts that eliminate extra steps.

If you're managing this type of employee, remember that when relaters are in training for a job, they favor one-on-one, hands-on instruction with a real live human being, starting at the beginning and ending at the end. By learning each step, they gradually become more comfortable with their functions. During training and in other newer situations, relaters tend to observe others for a longer-than-average time. They won't begin a task until they're convinced they can accomplish it.

Plan to be prepared when you interact with relaters. Have a step-by-step list of procedures or a detailed schedule at your disposal. Relaters need to feel secure in their mastery of procedures until their actions become "second nature" and can be done more routinely. At the same time, they prefer a pleasant and patient approach while they learn what's expected of them.

When you give advice to relaters, allow plenty of time to explore their thoughts and feelings so you can understand the emotional side of the situation. Relaters usually express their feelings less directly, so draw them out through questioning and listening to their responses. Bear in mind that this personality type tends to balk at sudden change, whether the change is good or bad. The key point is that their stability-motivated state is disrupted by the unknown. You can help reduce their fears by showing how specific changes will benefit them.

When you must correct relaters, reassure them that you only want to correct a specific behavior. Relaters tend to take things personally, so be sure to keep the conversation focused on the behavior and its appropriateness, and not on blame or judgment of the person. If the problem involves a procedure, help them learn how to improve it. Point out, in a nonthreatening way, what they're already doing right, even as you emphasize what needs changing.

When you praise relaters, mention their teamwork and dependability. However, be aware that effusiveness can arouse their suspicion. Stick to praising what they've done rather than more abstract or personal attributes. Communicating with relaters involves working to stay organized, and moving forward steadily but slowly. Make sure they both understand and accept what is being said.

When problems and decisions arise, tackle only one subject or situation, and go through it one step at a time. Before moving on to other items, make sure the relaters are ready, willing, and able to do so.

If you are a relater, stand up for yourself when others become insistent or even belligerent. Respond more favorably to required changes. Occasionally, vary your schedule and try new things. Expand your circle of acquaintances by participating more frequently in activities with new people. Respond somewhat less sensitively to others and even confront them once in a while. Consciously allow the occasional disruption of your peace and stability.

## Socializers: Traits

Socializers are friendly and enthusiastic, and they like to be where the action is. They thrive on admiration, acknowledgment, compliments, and applause. They want to have fun and enjoy life.

Socializers tend to place more priority on relationships than on tasks. They influence others in an optimistic, friendly way, and they focus on positive outcomes. Often, they're not as concerned about winning or losing as they are about how they look while they're playing the game. A socializer's greatest fear is public humiliation or appearing uninvolved, unattractive, unsuccessful, or unacceptable to others. The socializers' primary strengths are their enthusiasm, persuasiveness, and friendliness. They are idea people who have the ability to get others caught up in their dreams. With great persuasion, they influence others and shape their environments by building alliances to accomplish their results. They are risk takers, and they base many of their actions and decisions on intuition.

Their weaknesses are impatience, an aversion to being alone, and a short attention span, which causes them to become easily bored. With little data available, socializers tend to make sweeping generalizations. They may not check everything out; they assume someone else will do it. When taken to extremes, socializers' behaviors can be seen as superficial, haphazard, erratic, and overly emotional. Their need for acknowledgment can lead to self-absorption. They have a casual approach to time, and they often drive the other personality styles crazy with their missed deadlines and lateness. Fun-loving, life-of-the-party socializers can be undisciplined, forgetful, too talkative, and too eager for credit and recognition.

Socializers are often hired as sales personnel, public relations specialists, talk show hosts, trial attorneys, social directors on cruise ships, hotel personnel, and various other glamorous or high-profile positions.

## Interacting with Socializers

Socializers may need your help in focusing their abilities. With their energy and enthusiasm, socializers may get involved with so many different activities that they may accomplish goals with a flourish. They may also show flurries of activity, but not actually accomplish the desired outcome in the most efficient way. Managers and coworkers can help channel that energy and enthusiasm with tactful reminders and hands-on assistance with prioritizing and organizing assignments so that the entire workplace functions more smoothly.

Socializers like to envision the big picture. Generally, they are not well motivated by being given many facts and details. They respond better to capsule summaries of what you plan to cover. For this behavioral type, emotions rule. This doesn't mean that they never use logic or facts, but their feelings and emotions come first, and they dislike conflict. If you disagree with a socializer, try not to argue; explore alternate solutions instead. When you reach an agreement with socializers, iron out the specific details concerning what, when, who, where, and how. Then document the agreement with them because they naturally tend to forget such details. When you want to motivate socializers, remember that they like special packages and a little something extra to inspire them to go the whole nine yards. Show them how they can look good in the eyes of others.

When you compliment socializers, deliver direct, personal, positive comments. Mention their charm, friendliness, creative ideas, persuasiveness, and/or appearance—or better yet, all of the above. When a manager has to correct a socializer, it must be done in a positive way. When stress hits socializers, they prefer to look the other way and search for more positive, upbeat experiences. They avoid problems as long as they can. If the pressure persists, they tend to walk away from the problems. Let these individuals know specifically what each challenge happens to be. Define the behavior that can eliminate it, and confirm the mutually agreed-on action plan, *in writing,* to prevent future misunderstandings. Because they prefer to keep conversation light, avoid what they view as negative or distasteful approaches.

When you communicate with socializers in a selling situation, be prepared to listen to their personal feelings and experiences. They have a need to be expressive and to share their emotions with others. Their style requires open and responsive interaction with others. When socializers are making decisions or solving problems, they'll want to avoid a discussion of more complex, negative-sounding, or otherwise messy situations. It's difficult for them to feel positive or agreeable with you or anyone else under these circumstances. In making collective decisions, they'll be open to suggestions that will allow them to look and feel good and will not require a lot of difficult follow-up details or long-term commitments.

If a situation calls for delegating to socializers, make sure to receive a clear agreement. Set up checkpoints and periodic feedback times to avoid long stretches with no progress reports. Otherwise, socializers may lapse into their natural way of doing things—spontaneously completing particulars that make them feel good, and postponing less stimulating tasks, especially those that involve follow-up and checking. Socializers often come up with plenty of ideas, but they're not necessarily accompanied by the means or intent of carrying them out. It's up to you to steer them toward ways of ensuring the implementation of those ideas.

If you are a socializer, attend to key details and improve your follow-through efforts. Monitor your socializing to keep it in balance with the other aspects of your life. Write things down, and work from a list, so you'll know what to do when. Prioritize your activities, and focus on tasks in the order of their importance. Become more organized and orderly in the way you do things. Do the less appealing tasks of the day early. Pay more attention to the time management of your activities. Check to make sure you're on course with known tasks or goals.

Let's wrap up this section on personality types with a story that conclusively drives home the differences among the four basic styles. Many years ago, in the reign of Louis XIV of France, four noblemen were accused of committing a very serious crime. They were put on trial and, although they protested vehemently about their innocence, they were convicted and sentenced to death on the guillotine.

For the fateful day of execution, a special guillotine had been constructed so that all four could be beheaded simultaneously. The four noblemen—one a thinker, one a director, one a relater, and one a socializer—were placed in position for the execution, and upon receiving word from Louis XIV, the executioner swung his ax, cut the rope, and the blade descended rapidly toward the necks of the noblemen. Just as the blade touched their necks, it jammed. It was seen by Louis XIV as a sign from heaven that the noblemen were truly innocent, as they had protested during the trial. So the king set them free.

As they were freed, each nobleman expressed his appreciation in a different way—and very much according to his own individual style. The first one freed was the director. As he got up from the guillotine, he looked at everybody and said, "I told all of you I was innocent! Now maybe the next time you'll listen to me when I tell you something! And Louie, let me tell you something: I'm suing!" The second person freed was the relater. He went right up to the executioner and said, "I know this wasn't your fault. I want you to know that I'm not going to hold it against you. Would you like to come over for dinner on Sunday?" The third person freed was the socializer. He jumped up, looked at everybody, and said, "Let's party!" The final person freed was the thinker. As he was getting up, he looked up at the jammed guillotine blade and said, "I think I see the problem."

## Twenty-Eight Ways to Sell Smarter

Studies of consumers who buy and consumers who don't buy products and services in a sales situation show a number of things that sales professionals can do *during the sales process* to influence prospects to buy.

The following twenty-eight research-based factors will help improve your sales performance in a number of basic areas. By selling smarter, you can significantly improve your productivity.

1. *Resell to existing clients.* Your best source of prospects is your current client list. Research shows that seven in ten buyers will buy again from the same sales representative if they are happy with their purchase.

2. *Build up acquaintances.* Your most approachable prospects (and the prospects who are most likely to buy from you) are those who are familiar with you and with your services.

3. *Make a good first impression.* Research shows that 96 percent of all prospects are much aware of a sales professional's appearance; and more than half "form definite opinions of sales professionals from their appearance."

4. *Make an appointment.* Dropping in without an appointment hurts a sales professional's chances of making a sale more than any other type of approach.

5. *Make your true identity and purpose clear.* You can increase your chances of making a sale by honestly and favorably introducing yourself, describing your company, detailing what you do, and explaining your purpose for making the contact.

6. *Approach in person.* Talking to prospects face-to-face is a more effective way to secure appointments than are direct-mail and telephone approaches.

7. *Have in mind an idea that fits the prospect's needs.* Sales professionals sell ideas, not just products. Because

different types of prospects buy different ideas, the key is to know your market.

8. *Build rapport with the prospect.* Listen. Be polite. Never challenge an opinion; instead, look for areas of agreement. Always show an interest in your prospects, no matter how unusual or ordinary they may be.

9. *Conduct interviews in your own office.* Not only are interviews in your office more efficient, but prospects are slightly more likely to buy when the interview takes place in your office.

10. *If your product is for a household, have both spouses or partners present during the interview.* Most major decisions in two-person households are made jointly. In fact, the buying rate in such households is higher when both residents are included in the interview than when only one person is interviewed.

11. *Don't worry about requests to have other persons attend the sales interview along with the prospect.* The presence of another person—a relative, a lawyer, an accountant, or a family friend—actually improves the buying rate.

12. *Don't shy away from competition.* When considering a purchase, only one in four consumers have discussions with more than one sales professional selling a similar product. Consumers who do make comparisons are more likely to buy.

13. *Sell on a needs basis.* Prospects whose needs have been programmed are more likely to purchase than are prospects whose needs have not been programmed.

14. *Emphasize quality.* Prospects are more likely to buy if quality is emphasized than if savings are stressed.

15. *Be objective.* Never sacrifice objectivity for your own personal interest. Prospects who detect that you are placing your self-interest ahead of their interests are unlikely to buy from you.

16. *Present several different choices.* By presenting more than one solution, you allow prospects to exercise their need to feel in control.

17. *Recommend a specific type of product.* Prospects want latitude to make informed choices, but they also want to know what you sincerely believe is the best choice for them. Research indicates that when buyers buy, the product that the sales professional recommends is purchased almost 90 percent of the time.

18. *Make sure the prospect perceives that the products or services you recommend are adequate.* If prospects don't feel good about the products you recommend, they won't purchase them.

19. *Provide adequate and correct information.* Sales professionals must know how to present technical information in a clear, easy-to-understand manner; how much information to present; and how to answer questions (or at least where to find the answers).

20. *Discuss the incidentals.* Little things often sway a purchase decision. Where appropriate, discuss product specifics, including warranty information, product updates, and so on.

21. *Be thorough and helpful when discussing costs.* A majority of prospects ask questions about costs, and you can make a very favorable impression by how completely you satisfy their concerns.

22. *Avoid jargon.* Jargon in a sales situation doesn't impress anyone; it only confuses prospects.

**23.** *Educate prospects.* When consumers understand a product, they are more likely to buy it. Before you can get prospects to say "Yes," you must hear them say, "I understand."

**24.** *Be patient.* Pressure never sells. Most products are sold in two or more interviews, and research shows that buying rates increase with each subsequent interview.

**25.** *Make prospects feel that they are getting their money's worth.* Assure prospects that their money is well spent, and periodically reinforce the sale. Don't let customers forget the wisdom of their purchasing decisions.

**26.** *Provide service.* Customers who receive satisfactory service are much more likely to buy again from you than are customers who receive little or no service.

**27.** *Become the preferred sales representative.* One the most important research findings is this: When a prospect considers you his or her personal sales representative, the chances of a sale *and* of repeat sales improve greatly.

**28.** *Be a quality sales professional.* To a prospect, the quality of the sales professional is more important than the quality of the company he or she represents, the quality of the product purchased, or the cost of the product.

# Chapter 3

# Breaking Slumps

The bane of all sales professionals is the slump—a period of time when, in spite of all efforts, no sales are made. Slumps can end sales careers, but it isn't necessary to surrender to a slump. In fact, the best salespeople are adept at breaking out of slumps. Here are their best ideas.

## The Ten Career Traps for Sales Veterans

If you've been in sales for quite a while, certain problems may develop that can impede progress in your career. We identify ten dangerous traps facing experienced sales professionals. But before presenting these traps, let's discuss why the sales career is so unique.

Here's a mind jogger: Why did you become a sales professional in the first place? People in sales will almost universally respond that they were looking for independence, compensation commensurate with their talent and effort, and an opportunity to reach people. In short, they wanted a chance to be "captain of their own ship" and to guide their own destiny. Today, they want the chance to earn what they are worth on a level playing field and the ability to do something that makes a difference in their customers' lives. Taken together, these add up to a desire for personal freedom through their sales career.

How can you capture the benefits of this career? The answer lies in the development of a substantial client base. What is a client base? Clients are defined as "people with whom you have an ongoing relationship based on a consultative selling philosophy." They are people who identify you as their main contact for the product or services you sell, and who will buy repeatedly, over time, if you develop and nurture a long-term professional relationship. In essence, a client base is a reservoir of repeat sales, and each repetition tends to be easier, faster, more lucrative, and generally more fun. Without a client base, your efforts become an ongoing scramble for new sales. A growing client base brings with it financial success, security, reduced anxiety, and the personal freedom that all sales professionals seek when they enter the sales field.

In the final analysis, each of the 10 traps described here is actually an impediment to the building of your client base. By taking a look at the traps, perhaps you can shine a light into the dark corners of your sales practices and identify some genuine opportunities for you to get what you really want from your career.

## 1. Abandoning Your Client Base or Client Building for the Pursuit of Big Sales

Of course you want big sales; it's part of human nature to want to make money. Big sales are particularly alluring because they offer a genuine opportunity for business leverage. Real freedom, though, comes from a substantial client base, a large reservoir of repeat sales. Focusing exclusively on the big hit, rather than on systematically adding to your client base, puts you in the position of running a very high-risk business.

Sales professionals tend to rationalize the big-sale mentality with excuses. How often have you heard sales veterans say, "I have been in the business for a long time. I'm much more intellectually and financially sophisticated than I was when I came in." This, of course, is true. But then there's a tendency to add, "I don't really want to deal with lesser sales cases anymore. I have earned the right to deal with only large cases."

The problem is that the ability to make easier, more lucrative repeat sales leads to freedom. If you give all your attention to larger cases, many of them will be one-time sales. You'll make the sale but you won't add to the reservoir of repeat sales in your client base. This tack gets to be dangerous after a while, because soon there are no more clients to make repeat sales to. In fact, you're essentially forced to round up a new sale all the time, rather than having the financial reassurance of repeat sales from your client base.

Another problem tends to lead to the abandonment of client building as a philosophy: Most new clients tend to be younger in age. Many of these clients are *naïve*. They believe they understand the products and services you sell, and, being young, they're naturally very optimistic. They honestly believe that they know what they want and what they are talking about—and, in some cases, they are right! Perhaps life hasn't beaten them up yet; consequently, they don't fully appreciate the wisdom of veteran salespeople. As a veteran, you will say, "I don't know if I want to work with these people; they're not as much fun to deal with. They don't seem to respect my experience; they think they know it all." Again, this can lead you away from client building and turn your sights toward the big case.

The solution is twofold. First, you need to keep your referred-lead prospecting, personal observation, and marketing skills sharp so that you are constantly being introduced to quality people. Second, after meeting or actually selling to these people, you must operate within an organized client-contact program that prompts you to contact them at least twice a year.

## 2. Discontinuing to Take Complete Facts

One of the things that happens to professionals is that, after they have done a certain task for a long period of time, they become very proficient at it and may slip into the trap of saying, "You

know, after only a few sentences, after just listening to just a little bit of what prospects say, I'm pretty certain I know where it's
all going. I know what they're going to say, what the problem is,
and what the solution is."

This approach involves an incomplete diagnosis. You're not
really gathering all the information, and you'll tend to sell your
favorite idea rather than listening to get the complete situation
from the client.

You'll also interrupt the opportunity for bonding with your
clients. When you listen and pay particular attention to their
feelings, they begin to feel a special bond with you. If you short-
circuit that process, then you not only may miss certain needs that
are there—different sales that are possible—but you also interrupt
the bonding process and weaken the relationship. There really is a
double danger here: (1) you miss uncovering all of the prospect's
needs (hence, potential sales opportunities), and (2) you fail to
create the bond that leads to a trusting, long-term, professional
relationship.

The solution is pretty straightforward. Dust off those old but
excellent skills that served you so well in the past. Get a little
more organized, and prepare to take facts with the same caring
and thoroughness that a quality family physician would exhibit
when taking a medical history. Utilize a "user-friendly" stan-
dardized form for your fact-finding, to ensure that you cover all of
the important areas. Make sure that your information-gathering
approach moves professionally toward the collection of complete
facts. Conclude by developing a summary statement (a needs
analysis) with your prospect, to lay the groundwork for repeat
contact and future sales.

## 3. Confusing Being Busy with Being Productive

Anxiety, caused by the unrelenting requirement for prospecting,
impacts everyone in sales. Salespeople always have to be looking

for new clientele as they engage in client-building activities. Most salespeople would like to escape this ongoing task. Continually retaining a "prospecting mentality" is challenging, to say the least. Some sales veterans get so tired of this pressure that they unconsciously begin to avoid the process—even as they rationalize the slowdown by saying that they are, in fact, prospecting. When this happens, they begin to fill up their time with social, professional, or community service projects. In this way, they fool themselves into thinking, "Well, I'm very busy and I'm involved with lots of activities that will pay off with business someday."

If this is happening to you, you may actually feel good because you are meeting your needs for recognition. Sales professionals often rationalize their avoidance of the anxiety of prospecting by telling themselves, "I'm a successful person. I've worked hard and have been given a lot from my profession, my community, my church, and so on. Now I want to give something back to the industry and the community."

It's here that you have to be careful. Of course, you should give something back to the industry you work in, or to your community. But you need to candidly evaluate your actual motivation. A commitment to extensive service projects can be motivated more by an avoidance of the tougher tasks of the business than by a desire to serve.

One of the best remedies for avoiding all of these traps is to join a client-builder group. Monthly meetings with your peers are a wonderful way to get objective feedback from people who know the business and who care about you. In many instances, the only people who can keep a sales veteran on track are the members of his or her client-builder group. Maintaining the proper balance between the genuine fulfillment that comes with community or professional service and the demands of building a business presents a serious challenge. Remember, you help people tremendously in your business as well. Be aware of the potential danger in a tendency to avoid real prospecting by filling up your time with other behaviors that seem fulfilling but are not very productive for your bottom line.

## 4. Failing to Sustain Client Relationships

As you look for big sales opportunities, which is another very natural activity, there is sometimes a tendency to lose touch with the client base that you have already developed. You may think, "I'm not sure other sales are there; besides, I am now going to be operating in a different marketplace at a different level. I haven't spoken to some of these people for quite a while, and calling now might be somewhat awkward. Maybe I'll contact them later, if things get tough."

The problem is that by not staying in touch through a client-contact system, you drift away. If your ideas for very sophisticated sales situations don't work out—for whatever reason—and you then go back to your original client base, you may find that a lot of it has eroded. This is a real danger. Genuine personal freedom in your career comes through having a large, high-quality client base that is constantly refreshed with new people and nurtured through regular contact.

## 5. Avoiding an Obvious Sale

This may sound odd. Why would a salesperson avoid an obvious sale? Possibly because he or she has decided to sell only predetermined products or services (and prospects do not want or need them). There is danger to the predetermined-products approach. Prospects will see through your motives and concluded that you are working on your own agenda, not theirs. Consequently, you experience a twofold loss. You lose not only the obvious sale that you should have made easily, but also the long-term trust that had been anchored in your initial sales approach. There is a natural tendency for sales professionals to try to sell the latest, greatest product. But that's not always what prospects want. Take the path that offers the least resistance, and then rationalize the trip. This, in the long run, is a win–win situation.

## 6. Failing to Delegate to an Assistant

As you build a client base (depending on what business you are in), the service work on that clientele can continue to grow and grow. If you don't delegate this work to an assistant, it will have to be done by you. Sooner or later, you'll be spending the majority of your time completing lower-wage work, rather than the higher-wage work of a successful sales professional. What is worse, you may become so tired from this workload that you have no motivation or energy left to do the important work of building and developing your client base. Without an assistant, your sales skills will slowly die from service-work strangulation.

Some people are reluctant to delegate because they are "control freaks." Sales professionals tend to want to remain in complete control of everything. Maybe you were burned by others' oversights or mistakes in the past, and you have vowed to never let that situation happen again. In essence, you are afraid to trust an assistant. The question is: How much are you willing to pay in order to indulge this fear? What is this fear costing you—in dollars, business, quality relationships, and health?

What can you do? This is a genuine opportunity to change your operation and gain some leverage. First, it is important to regularly set aside some working capital to finance the best assistant you can afford. If you can't afford a full-time assistant, then begin by sharing one with another sales associate. But don't neglect this key to growing your business.

When you hire an assistant, don't sabotage the opportunity by shortchanging the training you give. Additionally, consider the advice of another great salesperson: "The first responsibility of an assistant is to take over virtually all telephone dialing for the boss." The reason this advice is so powerful is that many salespeople are reluctant to obtain referred leads because they are apprehensive about actually calling the prospects on the telephone. Think about how easy it would be to obtain personal introductions if you didn't have to do the dialing! Remember, an assistant doesn't take any rejection personally. His or her success is related to certain skills, but it mostly depends on the power and influence of the person who gave the referral.

In a survey, top sales professionals consistently said that if they had to do their career over again, they would hire a quality assistant as soon as possible, even if they had to borrow the money for the assistant's wages.

## 7. Abandoning a Structured Day or a Structured Approach to Your Time

You've worked very hard for a number of years. During this time, and particularly in your early years, you probably had a lot of discipline and you operated with a certain amount of structure and ritual. But one of the things that attracts people to the sales business is independence, and, as a sales veteran, you have an increasing opportunity to enjoy that independence. At times, you drift away from the discipline that made you successful. You become almost toxic from what can be the sweet poison of the freedom that the sales business offers.

You might be thinking, "Should I not enjoy the freedom?" Of course you should enjoy it! The whole purpose of working hard is to be able to live one's life in one's own way. But don't throw the baby out with the bath water. Work with balance. During the periods you have designated as work time, work with structure and discipline. A law of farming dictates a balance between enjoying the fruits of the harvest and continuing to prepare the soil and plant for the future. Above all, continue to use the system that made you successful. There is a famous Zen saying: "When you walk, walk. When you sit, sit. But don't wobble!"

## 8. Failing to Develop Centers of Influence

This is a trap that can become a tremendous opportunity. There are two types of client building that you need to develop. One is your actual client base—people who will repeatedly buy from you. The other is a network of centers of influence—professional people in your market who will refer you to their associates. We all know that most big sales come through strong referrals, and these referrals often originate from your centers of influence.

In addition to your fundamental client-contact system, you might consider a "contact tickler section" devoted to the contact and development of relationships with these centers. If you haven't done that as part of your career development, finding larger sales cases has probably been difficult. You need a balance between larger and more moderate-size cases in order to have a strong business. To obtain this healthy balance without completely abandoning your client base, develop these professional advisers as centers of influence. In essence, they become your second client base.

## 9. Failing to Continue to Learn

What is the competitive edge of veteran sales professionals? They have more knowledge, and when they take a fact finder from a prospect, they are able to identify a much wider variety of needs. They can identify problems that a junior sales associate may not even see. If learning is your edge and you stop learning, you fail to keep up with your industry's changes, and you relinquish your competitive edge. If you combine this lapse with a tendency to shortcut the fact finder, you now have a double whammy. You suffer a decrease in knowledge or in staying up-to-date on the latest information, and, with a shorter fact finder, you're running the risk of missing a lot of opportunities for sales.

Continual learning sharpens your saw. Keep reading, join a study group, take courses, sign up for seminars, continue to be a top-flight professional. Knowledge translates into confidence and a better chance of crafting solutions to your prospects' needs. As you engage in this ongoing learning process, take the time to convert what you are learning into informational pieces to send to your centers of influence. You'll truly create a win–win opportunity for everyone.

## 10. Discontinuing an Annual Review of the Quantity and Quality of the Client Base

What really is the equity in your business? It is your client base—the repeat sales represented by the group of people with whom you have an ongoing relationship. It's important to make an annual analysis of exactly what you have in your client base. Otherwise, there's no confrontation with the truth about the real worth of your business.

An annual review can be a joyful chore when you realize you have a gold mine that you're not fully mining. You need to know the value of your business. What would you be willing to sell the client base for? That figure comes from making an annual review of the quantity and quality of your clientele.

The review process helps in other ways as well. It gives you a picture of the people you have been selling to, what they are buying, and whether you are filling your reservoir faster than you are draining it. It also helps you to identify your ideal prospect and to create the minimal acceptable profile for a new client.

Knowing that you will make an annual review of the quantity and quality of your client base also encourages you to recommit to client building and to keep accurate business records of your activity, production, and clientele. Know the facts of your situation, and take appropriate action. Without records and without proper assessment, you won't know the facts and you won't be able to identify the appropriate actions.

A sales veteran can easily fall prey to these 10 traps. No one sets out to do these things consciously; people just drift into them. The sweetener in your situation is that you can usually correct these problems rather quickly if you choose to.

Consider your strengths. You have great knowledge and experience. You are smart and tough, as your survival in the business demonstrates. You know how to sell the products and services that you are associated with. The flaw is that in fighting the daily battles you sometimes lose sight of the big picture of your career development. While you focus on the day-to-day struggles, these traps can sneak up on you. Slow down a bit, step back, and take a careful look at your situation.

## Psychological Contributions to Selling

Recent advances in psychological knowledge have afforded serious students of the sales profession a better understanding of the basic motivations of prospects and customers—the drives behind their wants, which induce them to take action. Everyone apparently wants something better. Individuals seem motivated to move from present levels of satisfaction to new and better ones— a fact that has doubtless contributed to humans' hierarchy of wants. Humans are indeed basically "wanting" individuals.

What makes a consumer want a particular item, or prefer one over another, is of great importance to you as a sales professional. For this reason, you are initially concerned with the dynamics of behavior. Only with this knowledge can you successfully practice the art and science of salesmanship; only when so fortified can you persuade people to buy your goods or service.

To gain some understanding of the dynamics of behavior, you must get some insight into the *mental process*. Without such insight, you can hardly proceed to a discussion of consumer behavior. The mental process is controlled by the brain, which receives nervous stimuli from both external and internal sense organs. The mission of the brain is to coordinate these various stimuli and then give directions to the various reactions.

The brain is the seat of all our consciousness, emotions, memory, judgment, and imagination. Every voluntary and involuntary activity of the body is controlled by it. In the brain, thinking takes place—and what an exquisitely complex mental achievement the power of thought is. The brain is where the most important and distinctive intellectual activities, such as comparison, identification, and generalization, take place. These are the essentials of the selling function. Most important is the capacity of the individual, through the activity of the brain and the thought process, to perform acts of judgment.

Closely related—and also of major importance to the sales professional—is learning, which is an intimate part of the mental process and the resultant acts of judgment. The learning process is especially important to the sales professional because it is related to habit, another part of the brain's activity. The relationship is as follows: The brain, through the thought process, provides motivation plus the capacity for recognition of what may provide satisfaction. It also produces the ability to take action—make a decision—based on available alternatives.

Sales professionals take this learning process one step further. They recognize that if the same need is felt again by a given buyer, and satisfaction has already taken place in the buyer's initial use of the particular product or service, the buyer will probably continue to satisfy his or her future need through the same product or service. In effect, the buyer has learned that use of the product provided the required satisfaction. Experienced and creative sales professionals relate their actions directly to this process of the buyer's learning. As a result of this knowledge, these sales professionals provide the buyers with appropriate information—reinforcement, over time, so that the buyers can arrive at subsequent decisions more readily and with less need for mental activity. This entire sequence is favorable to sales professionals' products. Sales professionals thus strive to move their buyers to a point in the learning process where they will almost automatically satisfy their needs by buying the professionals' products or services.

Dedicated sales professionals who can successfully move a buyer to the point of buying by habit have built for themselves and their company an established relationship that is a source of great satisfaction and profit.

One thing is certain: People with a brain are also *wanting* in nature, and their desires are almost insatiable. Throughout their lives, they always desire something, and, as a sales professional, you should recognize immediately that fulfilling their wants and desires is not a simple task. There is much more to it than the basic idea that everything is built on just a few primary drives, such as hunger, fear, and comfort. The passing of time, complicated by technological and social advancement, has made it vastly more difficult to satisfy individual and group needs. Responses today have become relatively specialized and complicated. A review of this important area is essential because only creative sales professionals who are thoroughly informed on this subject can lead buyers to new levels of satisfaction.

Coupled with this knowledge of motivation is another factor of great importance to the sales professional: Nobody buys a product or service as such. People spend their money in exchange for what a product or service *will do* for them; they trade their money for a benefit they need or want. Thus, a sales professional who wants business must show customers how a given product or service will be beneficial to them. Each product or service must perform some essential task that satisfies the individual customer's motivations. If you, as a sales professional, understand these facts, you can show your prospects how your products provide the right answers.

In the next section, you will see that one dominant buying motive is linked to numerous lesser motives, and sales professionals must be aware of them as well of certain other related considerations that will help them to understand what goes on in a buyer's mind. There may be no secrets to closing a sale, but sales professionals who recognize and understand the motivations of their prospects will have the beginnings of an effective presentation and a good demonstration.

## Basic Motivations

In any study of human motivation, it must be first admitted that any effort to compile a comprehensive listing or classification of basic motivations is theoretically unsound because the ways of identifying and classifying the various motivations are too numerous, and no single list has any inherent claim to being more valid than others. In considering the various classifications, psychologist Abraham Maslow wrote:

> . . . all the lists of drives that have ever been published seem to imply mutual exclusiveness among the various drives. But there is not a mutual exclusiveness. There is usually such an overlapping that it is almost impossible to separate quite clearly and sharply any one drive from any other.

As a creative sales professional, you would have to understand these various stages as well as the changes in preference and consumption patterns that each stage signals. The motivations of a bachelor are quite different from those of a married man supporting his wife and children, because of the difference in each man's needs and wants.

An important fact is too frequently neglected: The cycle of development may also be applied to an industrial company that grows and, because of its growth, develops needs that define a particular stage in its life cycle. Much careful attention, based on sound information and knowledge, must be given by sales professionals to these respective life cycles and the forces that affect them.

Several other problems relate to the subject of motivation. For instance, there are differences between stated and rationalized motivations; a person may say one thing and mean another.

In Vermont, winters are frequently quite cold and snowfalls are heavy. To cope with the need for snow removal, chloride salt is used. This remedy is most effective in accelerating melting, but it eats away automobile steel and chrome trim. Living room discussions among Vermont residents often focus on the foolishness of using chrome trim on cars. People will say, "Why don't automobile manufacturers use better judgment and cut down or eliminate trim?" One company made the mistake of taking such statements literally; it removed the chrome. Result? The complainants bought a competitor's car, which was splashed with chrome. Why? Because the chrome gave the car a certain flair and excitement—a most important feature when one hopes to receive the admiration and approbation of friends and relatives as the new vehicle is brought home.

Another problem involves customers with motivational conflicts. They would like nothing more than to fulfill a desire to dress in high style and enjoy the prestige that accompanies their wardrobe. The problem? They have lean pocketbooks and are therefore severely restricted in their buying decisions.

In actual practice, sales professionals are primarily concerned with those motives of their prospects or customers that can be appealed to successfully in the selling of their products or services. Most companies, to assist in this effort, provide a list of the principal motivations that can most frequently be appealed to in selling their products, and they indicate how sales presentations may be built around these points.

The information that follows is intended to create a framework for your further study and analysis of the subject of motivation. The ultimate goal is a better understanding of what moves the customers you serve and the prospects on whom you call (see Figure 3.1).

Although numerous lists and classifications have been published and widely discussed, it is indisputable that needs can be divided into two general categories: physiological needs and learned needs. Physiological needs are associated with hunger, thirst, sleep, sex, comfort, cold, and pain. These underlying needs result in a drive directed toward a specific goal, which the individual expects will relieve the need. The specific behavior that is instrumental in satisfying a physiological need may be a reflex action, a behavior that is instinctive, or a specific activity such as eating, drinking, or sleeping.

The second broad category of needs, *learned needs,* includes needs that are precipitated by tension that develops as a result of an individual's association with other people. Compared with physiological needs, learned needs draw much less agreement

*Need*
↓
Behavior (drive)
↓
Goal
↓
Relief of need

**Figure 3.1** The Motivational Process.

among behavioral scientists as to their specific conceptions and labeling. One widely accepted classification of learned needs groups them into three basic categories:

1. *Need for affiliation.* In the highly organized society that exists in the United States today, people are very interdependent; they are required to interact a great deal with one another. However, over and above their required associations, most people have a strong desire for companionship and a natural desire to give and receive affection. Relationships with other people are necessary to satisfy basic emotional needs.

2. *Need for achievement.* Many people are motivated to achieve, through their own efforts, high levels of performance, or to work hard to overcome adversity. Underlying this drive to excel is a high need for achievement.

3. *Need for power.* The basic goal here is to be able to control or dominate the behavior of others, often by striving for recognition or status in a group.

These categories have proven useful in a number of ways. Primarily, they have been successfully applied to the understanding of broad economic questions such as an individual's striving for the acquisition of wealth, or the manner in which individuals choose to spend their time and income. Because the allocation of time and income has direct relevance to marketing, these categories provide a structure within which market analysts can work toward the solution of certain problems, particularly those associated with decisions regarding alternative expenditures of large sums of money. . . .

The following list, although by no means complete, demonstrates how motivations can be identified and classified:

✓ Profit and thrift.

✓ Safety and protection.

✓ Ease and convenience.

✓ Pride and prestige.

✓ Sex and romance.

✓ Love and affection.

✓ Adventure and excitement.

✓ Performance and durability.

*The profit motive*—the desire for an excess of return over outlay—is one of the strongest motives in most people. Unfortunately, too many people consider it the only acceptable criterion of value, and they accept the immediate turnover of cash as the only worthwhile type of profit. When your customers are businesspeople, this will frequently be their key motivation, but if you are an especially good listener who can catch hints of secondary motivation, that may tip the scales to your product. Remember that if cash profit were the only criterion, evaluation of competing products would be a very cut-and-dried procedure, and competition would be an academic curiosity.

*Thrift* is another powerful motivation and can easily be the dominant one in a situation where income is fixed. To improve the management of their resources, adults and children have had thrift demonstrated to them as a worthwhile goal and a standard practice in our culture.

*Safety and protection* concern us because preservation of our families necessitates the utmost in effort and planning. To satisfy this basic motivation, people will struggle to make certain that the future measures they plan are complete and are carefully adjusted to meet any contingencies that may arise.

An example may be helpful. If a prospect comes in and shows a sincere interest in power brakes, talks about nothing but safety, and worries about the steering mechanism and the efficiency of the power brakes for safe stops, don't—because of *your* preferences—go into raptures about the 400-horsepower engine and the high speed you can reach in three seconds. Talk always in terms of the prospect's interests, not yours! Learn, right here and now, *it's what they like that counts.* To put it another way, "It's the taste of the fish, not the fisherman, that determines the bait."

*Ease and convenience* are two basic human motivations that produce strong drives. People want greater comfort and convenience in their lifestyle. The proliferation of labor-saving devices in the home is proof of this. Almost everyone is interested in minimizing the discomforts of life and injecting pleasure into daily routines.

*Pride and prestige* are urges of great magnitude; people have always possessed a desire for achievement and feelings of personal dignity. They strive for recognition from others.

As an example, suppose you are just completing your presentation to sell $30,000 worth of life insurance to a young executive. You now have the option of discussing the low, low premium or reinforcing his sense of pride in protecting his family's future welfare. Which way would you go?

*The romantic drive*—sex and romance—is found in young and old and can be used effectively to sell many different products and services.

*Love and affection* are related motivations that produce an intense and absorbing urge that seeks gratification. Prospects will overextend themselves to provide things that help to make their family's life more pleasurable and to minimize hardship for their loved ones.

*Adventure and excitement* are basic urges that impel people to travel to far-off places and to see new things. Many of us court the new; the excitement of something different exhilarates us. We like the things that especially stir and rouse in us a pleasant excitement.

For example, a travel agent who sold a coach seat in an airplane, a 12-by-12-foot hotel room, and two meals a day in Rome would be laughed out of the travel industry for failure to merchandise the adventure and excitement of a trip to that historic city.

*Performance and durability* are highly desirable qualities in the products people buy. The consumer expects products to last for at least a reasonable time. During its useful life, the product, whether it is a car, an appliance, a blast furnace, a house, or a computer, is expected to perform the work claimed for it. There may be some considerations that consumers will close an eye to, but they will never overlook an inadequate performance or a lack of the durability that was reasonably expected.

The effort here has been to demonstrate that everyone wants something; we are all motivated in some way. The important questions for you as sales professionals are:

✓ What does [or will] motivate these individuals?

✓ How can I utilize these motivations to make them want what I am selling?

We have illustrated a typical list of motivations, but you must also learn that attitudes and personality traits have a great influence on your actions. These are the factors that make this subject so complex. Any individual's behavior is the result of many forces, which is why all buyers or prospects do not react in the same way to the same motivations.

Our understanding can be helped by reference to the field of gestalt psychology, where individual stimuli are seen and interpreted in terms of the individual's own experiences. Accordingly, buyers should be looked on as human beings who are made up of more than their motivations. They have beliefs, prejudices, attitudes, education, experience, and, of course, environmental influences—plus expectations and social values.

Some additional classifications of motivations have, for many years, been a part of marketing literature. Knowledge of these classifications is appropriate, provided that you, as a sales professional, realize that whenever the word *motivation* (motive) is used, it is not the sole factor between a stimulus and a response on the part of your buyer. What takes place in the sales interview is affected also by, among other things, attitudes, the influence of other people, and personality traits.

Sales appeals have been sorted according to whether emotional or rational elements predominate. Probably everyone wants to appear to be rational in making his or her decisions. The real problem in this controversy is whether a purchase decision made by a prospect for purely emotional reasons can also have a rational purpose.

## Primary, Selective, and Patronage Motives

An additional classification describes motives as primary, selective, and patronage. A primary buying motive is one that induces prospects to choose, because of need or desire, some kind or class of product or service. For example, an individual may, for whatever reason, decide to buy a state-of-the-art computer for the claims department of his or her company. That reason, whatever its specific intent, is called the *primary* motive. Once the decision has been reached, the buyer must choose one particular brand from among those available on the market. The reasons that lead to or influence the purchase of one machine that is preferred above all others are *selective* buying motives. The difference between these two types of motives may be illustrated by: a person's decision to buy a new automobile. This decision may be based on:

1. The desire for better transportation than is now being enjoyed.

2. Dissatisfaction with the styling of the presently owned vehicle.

3. Family requirements dictating the need for a larger car.

Regardless of whether one or a combination of these reasons predominates, it falls in the category of the primary buying motives. However, the car finally chosen may be selected on the basis of appearance, horsepower, size, or any number of other features. The various inducements for purchasing a particular car, once the primary motive dictates car buying in general, fall into the class of selective motives.

*Patronage motives* stimulate the buyers of both consumer goods and goods for commercial and industrial enterprises to purchase from a particular store or company. Among these motives are:

- ✓ Price—Some customers favor stores or companies that they believe stress low price, others prefer those that feature better quality, even at a higher price. Both types of customers utilize price as a patronage motive.

- ✓ Reputation of the seller—Customers are often influenced by the reputation for reliability that a particular seller has built up over the years; this, then, is their patronage motive.

- ✓ Convenience of location—A nearby store allows convenient shopping; nearby suppliers or vendors probably offer dependable delivery service. Both are excellent reasons for patronage.

- ✓ Breadth of choice—Variety of selection widens the choice for consumers and offers the opportunity for industrial buyers to reduce their number of suppliers.

✓ Reciprocity—This practice of buying from others because they buy from you is a powerful patronage motive that is sometimes observed in commerce and industry.

✓ Services provided—The efficiency, variety, and breadth of services offered by a seller often have a pronounced influence on buyers and provide a very strong motive for patronage.

✓ Influence of sales personnel—Perhaps the strongest of all patronage motives is represented in the sales personnel in an organization. Whether they are clerks in a retail store or a company's personal representatives who call on prospects and customers, the sales professionals are the critical points of contact between an organization and its customers. In the mind of a customer, the sales professional *is* the organization.

*All* these patronage motives have some import in the business of selling.

You are now ready to synthesize your knowledge of the ultimate consumer and industrial buyer, and of how and why each buys. Both types of buyers, as you have already observed, have certain traits in common: They purchase to satisfy certain basic motivations. As was pointed out earlier, the ultimate consumer is also a rational buyer who is engaged in problem solving and thus has purposes that are often similar to those of counterparts in industrial buying. Consumers try to satisfy certain basic motivations: increase wealth, secure advantage, dissipate fear, secure approval, improve health, emulate, and dominate, to mention a few.

The purchaser of industrial and commercial products, on the other hand, is expected to buy for reasons of economy and thrift, consistency of output, adaptability and stability, or performance and utility. It is expected that the purchasing agent for business and industry will deal regularly with dependable sources of supply that can be tapped confidently. In commercial relationships, the important thing is to supply materials and services that satisfy the customer's needs. Supplies, equipment, and machinery must fulfill the logistical needs of quality, price, and time. The relationship of the industrial buyer to the seller may be a personal one, but disciplined rational behavior is still of primary importance.

It is equally important to emphasize that each person is actually several persons. The particular person a customer is depends on the function he or she is performing. A buyer in private life who is on a shopping mission to purchase anything from a new suit to a television set or a new home is best appealed to by motivations such as popular acceptance, pride, style, and, of course, rational support for his or her choices. When the same buyer is purchasing as an expert for a company, other motivations must be considered. The appeals that will trigger his or her motivations are those that emphasize utility, reliability, performance, capability, and the like.

What has just been said is hardly new. It was commented on many years ago, by a renowned organizational psychologist:

> Experience with the methods used by sales professionals in the solicitation of orders for individual goods has shown that, in the personal interview, appeals are frequently made to the emotional motives of the buyer. Sales professionals oftentimes find that executives from whom they are soliciting orders take pride in the appearance of their plant; the gratification of that pride can be aimed at a buying motive. In other stances in personal interviews, sales professionals of industrial goods seek to arouse the spirit of emulation as a means of receiving orders; they suggest to prospective customers a desire to "keep up" with other manufacturers who have installed a particular type of machine or have bought the sort of material that the sales professionals are striving to sell.

Rational motives, however, undoubtedly predominate heavily in the trade in industrial goods.

Because so very much of what has been written is devoted to the ultimate consumer, it would seem judicious for you to find out more about industrial buyers and how the selling procedures for this market differ from those we are familiar with as consumers.

Several years ago, a careful and intensive study was conducted involving three large companies and 175 industrial marketing executives who bought a variety of goods and services. The study showed that companies pass through eight stages— designated in the report as "Buy Phases"—and that although some of these Buy Phases may occur simultaneously, they tend to appear in the following sequence:

1. *Anticipation or recognition of a problem/need.* Realization that a problem exists and that it may be solved by buying a product or service.

2. *Determination of the characteristics and quantity of the needed item.* Usually done within the firm, but outside sources may be helpful in arriving at this decision. In this phase, the process of narrowing down the solution has begun.

3. *Description of the characteristics and quantity of the needed item.* This extension of the preceding phase involves setting down a specific description of the item.

4. *Search for qualification of potential sources.* Self-explanatory: the outside sources that supply the product are carefully evaluated.

5. *Acquisition and analysis of proposals.* This may be a routine step or it can involve a complicated series of proposals and counterproposals running over several months.

6. *Evaluation of proposals and selection of suppliers.* Analysis of offers and possible further negotiation on price, terms, delivery, and other details.

7. *Selection of an order routine.* Includes both external aspects—preparation of purchase order, and follow-up activities—and internal aspects—reports to the using department, and inventory management.

8. *Performance feedback and evaluation.* Formally or informally, an evaluation of how well the product or service solved the problem and aided the performance of the supplier.

We have talked of many things that relate to psychology and motivation. You have learned that regardless of whether one is selling to the consumer or to the industrial buyer, the approach must be on an individual basis. Every prospect you see is different in certain respects. Your objectives as a sales professional are always: to isolate, appeal to, and satisfy the basic motivation of the individual buyer. You must be guided by the realization that people trade their dollars for what a product or service will do for them or for their company. Will it satisfy their needs and wants? Our brief discussion of perhaps the most advanced system in the world—the human mind—has emphasized the need for careful and meticulous sales preparation, orderly presentation, and intelligible comparisons that have genuine meaning for the listener.

At the center of motivation is the individual who evaluates alternative courses of action and selects and defines goals. Some of the intervening influences in this process are:

✓ *Cognitive style:* individual differences in the ways people perceive the world.

✓ *Previous experience:* events that shape goals, motives, and habits.

✓ *Culture pattern:* practices that help to determine values, aspirations, and expectations.

✓ *Level of aspiration:* how high a person aims in any direction.

✓ *Expectancy:* what individuals think will be the result of their efforts.

✓ *Group membership:* rules and limitations that apply to all members.

✓ *Reference groupings:* standards that help shape values and goals, regardless of whether the individual is a member.

## The Fear of Self-Promotion

Let's begin here with a question: What do Geraldo Rivera, Larry King, Oprah Winfrey, and Dr. Laura Schlessinger have in common? The answer: They're natural self-promoters. Like topnotch sales professionals and empire-building entrepreneurs everywhere, they have the instinct to exploit opportunities to make themselves visible.

Recent studies have shown that, in our culture, the highest rewards go to the persons most willing to self-promote. Self-promotion comes naturally to some people. The rest of us engage in a constant emotional battle between our ambition to reach for the top and our reticence to appear immodest, too forward, or too aggressive. That reticence and all the self-limiting habits of thought, feeling, and action that conspire to inhibit us from soliciting recognition for what we do well constitute "the fear of self-promotion."

When the fear of self-promotion emotionally interferes with a sales manager's ability to recruit top-quality sales professionals, it's called "recruiting reluctance." And, when it exerts a spirit-crushing emotional limit on the number of contacts a sales professional is able to initiate with prospective buyers, it becomes "call reluctance."

For some sales professionals, call reluctance means the inability to comfortably use the telephone to prospect. For others, it means discomfort prospecting face-to-face. For still others, it means being unable to comfortably do either. Perhaps you know a sales associate with that problem. Perhaps you manage one. Perhaps you are one.

Unlike some clichés, like the now discredited "fear of rejection," the fear of self-promotion and the related reluctances are not lighter-than-air marketing slogans. They have an objective existence, which means that they exist whether you believe they do or not, and their presence is measurable in direct consequences. Let's look at just a sample of those consequences.

Studies of the monetary earnings of sales professionals across many industries have indicated that those who still struggle with call reluctance averaged five times less per year than those who had overcome the problem during the same time period. (Both groups were essentially equal in talent, ability, motivation, intelligence, preparation, and experience.) To add insult to injury, the call-reluctant group had invested far more time and money learning what to do. They were just emotionally unable to allow themselves to apply what they knew.

If you've attended all the seminars, read all the books, and listened to all the motivational cassettes, and still suffer from unrewarded competence, then call reluctance could be the missing ingredient in your performance equation.

A few years back, after many psychological studies pertaining to call reluctance in sales professionals and their managers had been completed, a contrast study was conducted on non-sales populations. The logic works this way: If you've been studying the effects of cold weather on performance, it sometimes helps to contrast your data with some warm-weather effects on performance.

The contrast study examined the number of promotions and the dollar amount of salary increases earned by administrative management personnel over a five-year period. The far-reaching implications of the results could not be foreseen by the researchers.

The administrative managers who were promoted the most often and received the biggest pay raises did not turn out to be those who were most technically competent. Instead, the recognition and money flowed to those who were most willing to make visible whatever competence they had.

The relationship between self-promotion and success in direct sales was self-evident. But administrative managers?! The researchers asked themselves, "Have we used the wrong experimental design? Was the sample used abnormal in some way? Was an error made in the data analysis? Should we try this again?"

And they did try again—this time, with highly technical groups: systems analysts and systems engineers in the data processing industry. But the same conclusion surfaced again. The systems analysts and systems engineers judged to be best at their jobs were not necessarily those who were most technically competent. They were those who were most willing to promote the competency they had.

Two very important conclusions can be drawn here:

1. Call reluctance is not felt only by sales professionals; it can neutralize almost any career.

2. The first place where a person is most likely to feel call reluctance is not in a nervous stomach or a tight chest. Call reluctance is most likely felt first in the wallet.

In some industries, call reluctance has been all but eliminated. In others, it's about as bad as it has always been. The difference seems to lie in the ability of the industry—especially the sales managers in that industry—to tolerate the complex nature of call reluctance. In its general form, the fear of self-promotion, it inhibits everything from asking for a raise to taking credit for a job well done. But when call reluctance latches on to sales professionals, it is far more damaging. Its full force emotionally interferes with the number of sales calls a sales professional can make on a given day, and, to confuse matters further, it can assume eleven different shapes!

Here are the eleven characterizations of people whose sales careers have been held hostage by call reluctance.

**1.** *Doomsayers.* These people have one of the most lethal forms of call reluctance. Doomsayers habitually dwell on the things that can go wrong. Prospecting on the best of days can be difficult for anyone. Trying to prospect for new business while on continuous "red alert" is a behavioral self-contradiction. Doomsayers are not likely to be represented in large numbers in the Million Dollar Round Table.

**2.** *Overpreparers.* Members of this group habitually use preparation—waiting for new sales supports, or being preoccupied with planning—as an excuse for not making sales calls. When overpreparers begin to experience trouble in sales, some transfer to the corporate headquarters, where they indulge their passion for preparation by habitually holding or attending meetings. There are meetings on planning, meetings on goal setting, and even a few meetings on how to hold a meeting! The results can be catastrophic. When this form of call reluctance reaches high enough in the corporate hierarchy, overpreparation can become institutionalized. The behavioral focus on bottom-line sales can deteriorate into endless rhetoric about sales, delivered by support people who are not even accessible to the salespeople they are supposed to be supporting. (Theologians who are searching for evidence in support of life after death should observe overpreparers in company home offices, around three o'clock on a Friday afternoon.)

**3.** *Hyperpros.* Hyperprofessionals habitually dribble away vast amounts of energy denying that they have call reluctance and making excuses for the calls they are not making and the new business they are not closing. (You've heard about the large account that's always "right around the corner.") Hyperpros may be high-caliber veteran sales professionals, but they are often not nearly so productive or happy with their sales career as they could be. Many of the skills and talents they have forged on the anvil of experience get diffused instead of used. They engage in endless lamentations about unsalable products, unfavorable economic conditions, incompetent management, and insensitive colleagues. Instead of gravitating to the corporate office, hyperpros are inclined to become consultants.

**4.** *Stage fright sufferers.* Many high-level veteran sales professionals habitually limit their self-promotional activities to one-on-one presentations, and they avoid opportunities to promote their interests before groups because they have never learned to overcome their fear of speaking before groups, and nobody ever bothered to teach them. This form of call reluctance is entirely learned and can be easily unlearned.

**5.** *Separationists.* These individuals habitually fail to utilize the social networks and contacts available to them through their personal friends for fear of offending these people and losing their approval.

**6.** *Role Accepters.* These sales professionals are guilty of a chronic energy-sapping misuse of energy. They deny the private feelings of guilt and shame that they associate with their sales career and maintain a public façade of zealous professional over-identifications. (Secretly, they are ashamed of what they do.) They try to camouflage how they feel by rigidly trying to act and stay positive. It's usually only a matter of time before the efforts required to sustain the façade of positive certainty start to interfere with critical success-supporting behaviors such as prospecting. This type of call reluctance is highly contagious. It comes from emotionally buying into the public's stereotypes about what sales professionals are like and what they do—even though, intellectually, the afflicted sales professional knows that these stereotypes are not true. This form of call reluctance is found more frequently in the financial services industry than other industries.

In veteran sales professionals, researchers found what is called the "QWS" ("Quit While Succeeding") syndrome. Each year, many highly successful sales professionals abandon their sales career without warning or apparent reason. They just walk away. At the time of their resignation, many are enjoying very high incomes. They have not been production failures. Why do they quit? One answer echoes throughout the research studies: "The financial return no longer justifies the emotional investment." The emotional hassle referred to here is the continuous need for new business—a process these professionals secretly despise because of an unresolved role acceptance traceable, in many cases, to their very first trainer who interrupted a presentation and said, "We don't call ourselves *salespeople*." The new sales professional, soon to become a big hitter, learned to presume that selling must be bad or wrong or unacceptable in some form. Why else would it have to be disguised? The answer never came because the question was never actually asked. It got buried with other unfinished business, only to surface again in the QWS syndrome. Of all the debris that call reluctance leaves in its path, this is probably the most tragic because it is so avoidable and unnecessary.

**7.** *Yielders.* Yielders are like overcautious drivers who will not enter a freeway with the flow of traffic. Instead, they habitually pause, come to a complete stop, and yield their right-of-way to others. They are too busy waiting for just the right time, or just the right situation, to prospect for new business on a regular and consistent basis now.

**8.** *Socially self-conscious.* Sales professionals with this type of call reluctance emotionally designate certain segments of their market to avoid. They insist that they are afraid of no one, yet they habitually neglect to call on persons of wealth, prestige, and power, to protect themselves from being intimidated. In a nutshell, they are emotionally unable to allow themselves to aim high—to contact upscale centers of influence and gain access to the upscale people to whom they can sell upscale products and services. The result is often a catastrophic misalignment of human resources and market requirements.

**9.** *Emotionally unemancipated.* These sales professionals habitually fail to utilize the social networks and contacts accessible to them through members of their own family.

**10.** *Telephobics.* These individuals experience energy-sapping distress whenever they try to use the telephone to prospect for new business. (Face-to-face prospecting may be unimpaired.)

**11.** *Referral aversives.* These sales professionals become distressed when the opportunity to solicit referrals presents itself. Afraid of offending existing clients, or losing a just-closed sale, these sales professionals default on the bridge to their next sale by not asking for referrals.

This has been a brief, preliminary overview of the specific, career-threatening shapes the fear of self-promotion can take when it becomes call reluctance in sales professionals.

Why is type important, anyway? Type is important because knowing which form you have, or are predisposed to adopt, is the single most important thing you need to learn about call reluctance. From type, you forecast outlook, because some types are more resistant to correction than others, and one type is not curable at all! Identifying type points you toward specific things to do. Certain techniques work quickly and easily for some types of call reluctance and have no effect on others—or make them worse. A recent, faddish experiment with stress management proved disappointing for sales professionals with call reluctance because it was erroneously based on the assumption that call reluctance was one condition (like shyness or timidity) and would yield quickly and easily to one corrective approach. That error undoubtedly cost many sales professionals—and probably a manager or two—their sales careers.

Where does call reluctance come from? There are two sources. A couple of types are traceable to hereditary influences. They tend to run in families. The others are all learned, and some are highly contagious. That means that at some point, somebody, in some way—actively or passively, intentionally or unintentionally—taught us how to be call-reluctant. Most likely, we learned through prolonged exposure to someone, or some people, who had career-lethal levels of call reluctance. Who were they? Parents? Siblings? Friends?

Back in the 1980s, researchers conducted a study, using SPQ*GOLD—a special test that psychologists George W. Dudley and Shannon L. Goodson developed to measure call reluctance. Researchers studied the presence, severity, and type of call reluctance in a group of prospective life insurance sales professionals. At that time, they were no more and no less call-reluctant than anyone else. A few weeks later, after they had been selected to join the sales force of a branch where researchers had already had the opportunity to measure the managers and sales trainers, it was a different story. Not only did the new group begin to show signs of being call-reluctant, but the two type(s) that researchers were beginning to detect were exactly the types they had found in the management!

Continuing to measure, the researchers discovered the same two types in the regional vice president, then in the senior vice president of sales and marketing, and finally in the chairman of the board! "Ground zero" for call reluctance in the insurance industry may be the executive suite!

But who has the most call reluctance of all industries? The indelicate answer came from research again. What started out as a curiosity wound up as an embarrassment. The most likely candidates for call reluctance were the army of psychologists, consultants, motivational speakers, and other self-styled interpreters of sales professional behavior!

## Fear-Free Prospecting and Self-Promotion

It's a typical Monday evening at United Metro, Inc. Nancy, one of the company's top sales professionals, is at her desk. Now and then, she glances at a nearby wall clock. She knows that prospecting for new clients is crucial if she is to diversify and expand her client base. But that self-evident knowledge is no match for the chest-pounding fear she has secretly endured for years every time she tries to use the phone to prospect. Over the years, she has coerced herself to do what needs to be done. To her peers and colleagues, she is already highly successful. But Nancy knows better. She is keenly aware of the part of herself that has been persistently asking of late, "How much more could I produce, how much more would I enjoy my work, if I could prospect more comfortably on the phone?" She reflexively reaches for the phone. But instead of dialing a prospective buyer, she calls Ted, a long-time associate. It's a coping ritual. Her performance objectives will once again be subverted by a nice warm cup of coffee sweetened with lumps of the latest industry gossip.

Larry, an experienced sales professional, is a similar example. A man of fiery and fidgety temperament, he's been in his industry for a number of years. Undeniably dedicated, he is also competent, loyal, intelligent, and talented. But, year in and year out, the production of his sales organization remains remarkably unremarkable. Larry is fond of boasting that he can "call on any prospect, or recruit any sales professional" he wants to. And he can and does, as long as they are lower on the socioeconomic status ladder than he is. High-level sales professionals with high-level connections are avoided. Larry knows what to say and how to say it. But persons with wealth, prestige, or social connections intimidate him. "They're all SOBs," to hear him tell it. "I've been getting along fine without them for fifteen years, and I don't see why I need them now."

He's wrong. He does need them now. Recruiting high-profile sales associates is important. They are the tactical link between product and market for his company's new line of profitable upscale products and services. For some sales managers, this new emphasis would be a welcome change of direction. For Larry, and managers like him, it's that time again. Run or fight.

## Fear and Fearlessness in Selling

According to the stereotype, successful sales professionals are supposed to be oversocialized, overstylized, and absolutely fearless. Decades of "research" and armchair speculation have strengthened this stereotype through mindless repetition.

## "Research"

When you hear the word "research," your mind uncritically responds with images of white lab coats, thick volumes of obscure information, or cryptic mathematical formulations. But much that passes for knowledge about success in sales can be attributed to an altogether different use of the word. In many pop-psych books about success, research is a credibility tag formerly provided by footnotes placed in homage to Freud, Aristotle, and St. Augustine. What is meant by research? It may not be what the name implies. Research today often means little more than "I was interested enough in the subject to have read a magazine article about it," or "I recently attended a workshop," or "I talked to some people about it." Regrettably, much of the information about what sales professionals are like—or, more importantly, what *successful* sales professionals are like—is traceable to this variety of research. Very few organizations have sponsored formal, ongoing research conducted with sales professionals under controlled conditions. As a consequence, and despite opinions to the contrary, not much is known about what salespeople are actually like. Information about highly productive salespeople such as those in MDRT is even more sparse.

According to the pop-psych pamphleteers, highly successful sales professionals are "sociable," "uninhibited," "adventurous," and "forceful." But years of formal personality research have penetrated the cloud cover of overconfident smiles and practiced handshakes that characterizes some sales professionals and have revealed an aspect of the successful sales professional that is often unseen by less serious, interview-based studies.

Serious investigators have known since the mid-1970s that sales professionals vary considerably from their stereotypes. Using objective personality tests like the Sixteen Personality Factors Questionnaire and SPQ*GOLD, researchers have found that sales professionals are remarkably indistinguishable from non-sales professionals in terms of forcefulness, sociability, or social adventurousness.

What about fearlessness? It's a myth. Many successful sales-people, it turns out, are still struggling with a bone-shaking fear of prospecting, a fear that persists regardless of what they have to sell, how well they have been trained to sell it, how long they have been selling it, how successful they have been at selling it, or how much they believe in the product's worth.

An enormous number of Nancys and Larrys are out there. You may know one. You may *be* one. Each has an annoying, career-limiting "disease" that experts call *fear of self-promotion.* When this parasitic fear infects a sales professional's (or manager's) attitude about prospecting, it's called call reluctance. Contrary to popular stereotypes, a lot of sales *veterans* and their managers have it. The compulsive optimism and cavalier verbal gratuities the public often attributes to sales professionals in general are often just symptoms being displayed by a few sensitive people who are in emotional pain. It's their way of trying to hold their careers together with the sheer energy of their hopes.

## Hidden Menace

Every sales veteran knows that results are critically linked to the number of contacts initiated with prospective buyers. Figures vary with industries, products, and markets, but, generally, it appears to take about twenty-five contacts to get twelve responses, which result in five sales presentations and three closed sales.

Veteran producers already know those statistics. So what's the problem? Why don't more sales professionals (neophytes and veterans alike) produce at, or at least near, their actual level of ability?

Legions of otherwise capable sales professionals fail each year because they are unable to translate what they know about the relationship between prospecting and closed sales into goal-supporting prospecting behaviors. For example, one research project discovered that almost half of the people going into sales in a specific industry for the first time had undetected call-reluctant attitudes at the time they were contracted. In that industry, those attitudes don't remain silent for long.

A large percentage of all new sales professionals fail within their first year because they don't close enough sales. They don't close enough sales because they don't make enough sales presentations. They don't make enough sales presentations because they don't have enough prospects to make presentations to. They don't have enough prospects because of insufficient prospecting activity. Their prospecting activity is low because of fear, not fearlessness.

Many sales professionals are afraid to initiate contact with their own prospective buyers. For them, that fear on call reluctance is the missing link in their performance equation. It's the "social disease" of the direct-sales profession. Along with its staggering impact on turnover, call reluctance exacts a still heavier price. Research has shown that, regardless of industry, sales professionals with call reluctance produce up to five times less volume, new closes, and commission dollars than non-call-reluctant sales professionals with equal tenure.

Confirmatory research found this figure to be true within specific industries such as the financial services industry. But it doesn't stop there. A recent doctoral dissertation in psychology found that call reluctance also contaminates job satisfaction, making it difficult for call-reluctant sales professionals to enjoy their career, regardless of their tenure or current level of income. Call reluctance extorts an emotional and a financial ransom.

## Call Reluctance in the MDRT?

What about highly successful producers like MDRT members? They are not immune. On average, 40 percent of all veteran sales professionals experience one or more episodes of call reluctance severe enough to threaten their continuation in sales, despite their years of experience or current level of financial success.

Their struggle is reflected in the problem that psychologists call the QWS (Quit While Succeeding) syndrome. An unexpectedly high number of veteran sales professionals who quit or intend to quit while they are succeeding. In the past, researchers, along with other naïve investigators, thought that call reluctance was limited to inexperienced sales professionals. Veterans either did not complain or complained so loudly and so often that their genuine appeals for assistance were masked. Many enjoyed very high annual earnings. Some were MDRT members and award-winning sales associates within specific industries. All were presumed to be immune from annoying clientele-building problems like call reluctance. When the problem was suspected, it was verbally abstracted to lighter-than-air concepts like "midlife crisis," "burnout," or "stress."

Armed with formal tests, laboratory instruments, and even an interview or two, psychologists methodically tracked the problem. Common themes emerged. One was denial. Very few people—sales managers, close friends, colleagues, or even family members—knew call reluctance was still a problem. Another theme was compensatory prospecting. Here, prospecting efforts were shifted from emotional hot spots (like seminar selling, because of a fear of speaking before groups) to prospecting paths of lesser resistance. Typically, in compensatory prospecting, important market segments are neglected for purely emotional reasons that are often obscured by impotent excuses posing as rational explanations.

The third theme discovered was the most devastating to the call-reluctant sales veterans, their companies, and their industry. Without warning, sales veterans with QWS syndrome stepped completely out of character and resigned. As if on impulse, they quit the business many of them loved. Often, they vanished, dropping completely out of sight. Over the years, these QWS veteran producers were contacted and asked to help researchers understand why. Their common explanation was, "The financial return could no longer justify the emotional investment." Call-reluctant neophytes, they had learned how to prospect, but had never learned how to prospect for new business comfortably. Instead, many had been taught only how to cover up the problem by pretending to be positive. It was pure theater.

MDRT research found a number of productive pre-QWS syndrome sales associates on stage, playing the role of being positive. They had allowed themselves to become emotional frauds.

Of all the costs associated with call reluctance, the QWS syndrome is probably the most damaging. It is also the most unnecessary. In most cases, with a little sensitivity to the needs of the sales veterans and some workable countermeasures, their call reluctance is easily correctable.

## Genesis

Call reluctance is a career-threatening condition that limits what sales professionals can achieve by emotionally limiting the number of sales calls they are able to make. Some have trouble using the telephone as a prospecting tool. Others have trouble initiating contact with prospective clients face-to-face. Some have trouble doing both. All know how to prospect.

Call reluctance can be present at the onset of a career, or it can strike suddenly in a highly productive sales veteran. Its origins are multiple and complex. There is no single source like "shyness" to analyze, no single germ like "timidity" to destroy. But its origins can be reduced to three basic sources: (1) personality predisposition, (2) hereditary influences, and (3) environment.

Some forms of call reluctance tend to run in families and appear to be transmitted in the form of personality predispositions. Other forms can be traced to a single, traumatic, early selling experience. Sometimes, the cause is overtightened performance pressures. In a surprising number of cases, highly contagious forms of call reluctance are spread by the sales training process itself.

## In Their Own Image

Over the years, researchers have had the opportunity to measure the levels of call reluctance in many people *before* they began their sales careers. For example, psychologists spent a number of months measuring a group of prospective sales professionals. Six to eight weeks after being selected into an organization, they were measured again. As a group, their first set of scores showed no unusually toxic levels of call reluctance. But the results of their second test were a different matter. Not only did this group begin to show early signs of call reluctance, but the types of call reluctance they were beginning to show were the same two types that had been uncovered earlier in their sales managers and trainers!

Earlier studies done at the same company revealed that the types of call reluctance found in the sales managers and trainers were the same two types that were discovered in the regional vice presidents of sales—and in the senior vice president of sales and marketing!

Call reluctance was a silent epidemic in this company. The chief coping strategy, denial, had become institutionalized. Quite obviously, the call reluctance was still spreading despite efforts to eradicate it. For this company, and many others like it, the home office is ground zero for call reluctance.

## Mystery Religions

Most sales veterans learned, from a sales manager or trainer, early in their careers, how to cope with the demands associated with prospecting. Until recently, most of these well-intended managers impulsively reacted to call reluctance by desperately seeking the aid of priestly exorcists from the psychological fast-food industry. After being given a rich blend of ceremonial ritual, mysterious jargon, and evangelistic zeal, these managers were confidently assured that the offending fears would quickly yield to a more positive mental attitude, or be overpowered by a 45-minute inspirational cassette, or be soothed away by the gentle intonations of a subliminal stress-management tape. Having seen this response role-modeled early in their careers, many sales veterans still automatically sip from the same bottle of medicine when they experience pangs of fear associated with prospecting. How do you cope with prospecting today? In the same way as the trainers who originally trained you? Think back . . . .

Some sales veterans have matured in their profession without losing the added weight of frequently repeated misconceptions. "Call reluctance is unavoidable; everybody has some" is just one example. Others have been fatalistically colored by cynical sales managers or burned-out colleagues who were coping with their own unresolved case of call reluctance. How many times have you been exposed to this call-reluctant lamentation? "There's nothing you can do about it. It just comes with the territory. If you can't stand the heat . . . . "

What if you've read all the books, listened to all the cassettes, been to all the workshops, and are still stuck on the same old production plateau—still not earning what you know you're worth? Maybe it's not your products, your markets, your company affiliation, or general economic conditions. Maybe it's call reluctance. Here are some checkpoints for diagnosing whether you have call reluctance.

## Sighting the Target

Just recently, dealing with call reluctance was a frustrating, futile experience. The speakers' circuit reverberated with murky concepts and mindless platitudes like "fear of rejection" or "fear of failure." Cap pistols were deployed when heavy artillery was needed. Positive outcomes were sparse. Sales veterans and neophytes alike were stuck on production plateaus considerably beneath their talent, ability, and market opportunities. Many

industries suffered embarrassing sales-employee retention figures (which makes it doubly difficult for productive veterans to
be seen as mature professionals in a stable career).

## Charting the Course

The greatest single reason for the failures of the past was the ab-
sence of a compass. There was no coherent direction. Sales professionals lacked a workable definition of call reluctance, and
the vacuum was readily filled by cranks, charlatans, and chaos.
Desperate for solutions, but lacking a definition or a plan, sales
professionals squandered enormous amounts of money. In the
process, they looked and sounded like a battalion of color-blind
lawyers arguing about the color green. Threatened only with
high-sounding clichés spoken in low, churchly voices, call reluctance easily maintained its chokehold on production. According
to many MDRT members, it still does.

## A Systematic Approach

Dealing with call reluctance effectively is an orderly process. To
start, you have to distinguish the authentic article from other
prospecting problems that only look like call reluctance.

The best initial indicator of call reluctance is your prospecting activity: the total number of face-to-face selling interviews
and appointment-getting phone calls you make per unit of time,
relative to the number you should be making. The number you
should be making is determined by your own performance objectives and the size of your market. Easily quantifiable prospecting
activity is lawfully related to call reluctance.

Behavioral science sparkles from the speaker's podium. But
when you examine it closer, you find that it's quite ambigu-
ous. Its proponents are expounding enthusiastic speculations

masquerading as behavioral laws. Occasionally, behavioral scientists do find a genuine (and usually self-evident) law. The following law involves the relationship between prospecting activity and call reluctance:

> Call reluctance is always accompanied by low prospecting activity—that is, activity that is insufficient to sustain personal or career objectives, market potential, or personal ability.

> But look out. There's a catch. A high temperature may tend to accompany the flu, but the temperature by itself cannot be taken as positive proof that you have the flu. There could be other explanations. They must be ruled out before a diagnosis is complete and a medicine is prescribed.

Similarly, although low prospecting activity always accompanies authentic call reluctance, not all low prospecting activity is necessarily due to call reluctance. There can be other reasons, and they should be ruled out prior to diagnosing call reluctance and prescribing remedies.

## Three Essential Ingredients

Authentic call reluctance is indicated when low prospecting activity is accompanied by three essential conditions. First, you must be motivated. You must be internally energized. You must want to succeed in sales. Second, your motivation must be focused on at least one specific goal that is accomplishable in your present sales organization. Third, you must be self-obstructing. Your "want" is not making the trip to your goals intact. There's an energy leak. The wire leading to your goals is getting short-circuited. Instead of using their fund of physical energy (motivation) to prospect, call-reluctant salespeople use it to cope with prospecting. That's authentic call reluctance. It turns the opportunity to prospect into a grim and taxing emotional energy drain.

## The Great Impostors

If any of these three conditions is absent, you could still have prospecting problems, but they are not due to call reluctance. Cures aimed at correcting call reluctance will then have little effect because these supposed cures are call-reluctance impostors. There are three impostors: non-motivated sales professionals, misarranged goals, and outside energy draining problems. Let's review two.

If you don't make the calls you could and should be making because you are no longer motivated to do so, you're not call-reluctant—you are unmotivated. You either don't want to prospect, or you no longer want to meet the goals you set for yourself. For neophytes, the solution to this problem lies in more effective sales selection procedures. For veterans—who may have lost the motivational edge to perform at their best—the solution is more complex. Through the years, other things could have begun to compete for the limited supply of energy they can bring to their career each day. Problems with family members, problems with business associates, social obligations, and emotional setbacks all burn energy. Sometimes, these problems are situational. They disappear with the passage of time. At other times, they may be more pervasive and require the services of a professional. In neither instance is the drop in production due to call reluctance.

Let's look at another impostor that is typically misdiagnosed as call reluctance. Margaret is a highly motivated sales veteran. But her motivation is not properly aligned to the opportunities in her present sales situation. Though motivated, she either doesn't know exactly what she wants anymore, or she now wants success in a form that is not obtainable in her present career setting.

As a result, her prospecting activity has begun to deteriorate noticeably. It will continue to spiral downward as the difference between her personal goals and her current career situation increases. At a colleague's suggestion, she was recently interviewed by an ex-call-reluctant sales professional who has been reborn as a management consultant. Swaggering with overconfidence, he officially diagnosed Margaret as "call-reluctant" and prescribed megadoses of psychological pixie dust found in his new series of six overpriced cassettes. The results were predictable. No change. Why? Margaret was not call-reluctant to begin with. Her goals were misarranged. She was an impostor.

Call-reluctant impostors can be just as lethal to a direct sales career as the real thing. But they don't contain the three essential conditions for authentic call reluctance, and they don't respond to the remedies designed to correct call reluctance.

Is your career limited by call reluctance? Before you spend time or money on exotic cures for call reluctance, rule out other causes of low prospecting activity. Unfortunately, that may be easier said than done. Most approaches to assessing call reluctance in sales professionals fall woefully short. Typical assessment tests, for example, tend to be based on incorrect stereotypes like the ones discussed earlier. Most consider call reluctance worthy of only a footnote or a passing phrase. Few are able to distinguish authentic call reluctance from other causes of low prospecting activity, such as the four great impostors. And to make matters worse, authentic call reluctance has the eleven different forms previously discussed.

The assumption that one or two elemental notions—"timidity" or "stress," or the now discredited "fear of rejection"—lay at the roots of call reluctance evaporated in the face of new evidence. Instead of one or two neatly packaged concepts, psychologists now have eleven different forms of call reluctance.

Let's return to the earlier example. Nancy is a *telephobic*. She endures performance-limiting fear whenever she attempts to use the telephone to prospect. Like several of the call reluctance types, telephobia is a highly targeted fear. It only affects Nancy's ability to prospect on the phone; her face-to-face prospecting is unaffected. Because she has successfully compensated by emphasizing other forms of prospecting, her call reluctance has gone largely unnoticed. But Nancy knows it's there. Recently, she has started to seriously ask herself: "Is it worth it anymore?" Nancy is starting the process of psychological termination. If something is not done in the next few weeks, she will become a QWS syndrome statistic.

Larry, the second example, has a history of chronic *social self-consciousness* call reluctance. That's the opposite of target marketing. It's targeted avoidance of a segment of his market. Other segments may remain unaffected. Social self-consciousness is characterized by progressively shying away from prospects who have wealth, prestige, or power. It is highly contagious. Larry was infected by a "carrier," a contaminated sales trainer, early in his career.

## Ways of Curing Call Reluctance

Correlational studies have shown that the eleven types of call reluctance are separate and distinct entities. Each has its own developmental history, structure, and impact on prospecting behavior. Each differs from the others in terms of predictablity, preventability, and correctability. From the remedial perspective, type is critically important.

Why? Some types are much easier to work with than others. Doomsayers, for example, tend to be very time-consuming and, at best, can learn only to arrest their problem. Like alcoholics, doomsayers are never cured. Social self-consciousness, on the other hand, looks worse to the uninitiated than it really is. It's usually easy to correct once it's been properly diagnosed and the right techniques are applied. Table 3.1 summarizes the key

Table 3.1  The Eleven Types of Call-Reluctant Sales
Professionals: Behaviors and Cures.

| Call-Reluctant Sales Professionals | "Marker" Behaviors | Best Corrective Techniques |
|---|---|---|
| 1. Doomsaysers | Will not take social risks. | Threat desensitization. |
| 2. Overpreparers | Overanalyze, underacts. | Thought zapping, fear inversion. |
| 3. Hyperpros | Fear humiliation. Consider prospecting demeaning. | Fear inversion, thought zapping. |
| 4. Stage fright sufferers | Fear group presentations. | Threat desensitization, yellow dot, sensory injection. |
| 5. Separationists | Fear losing friends if business and friendship are mixed. | Negative image projection, thought zapping, thought realignment. |
| 6. Role accepters | Secretly ashamed to be in sales. Hold a negative stereotype about sales professionals. | Thought realignment, sensory injection, thought zapping, target reversal. |
| 7. Yielders | Fear being considered pushy. | Assertion training, thought realignment, yellow dot. |
| 8. Socially self-conscious | Only fear prospects who have wealth, prestige, or power. | Thought realignment, thought zapping, sensory injection. |
| 9. Emotionally unemancipated | Won't mix business and family, for fear of being considered exploitive. | Negative image projection, thought zapping, thought realignment. |
| 10. Telephobics | Emotionally unable to use the telephone for prospecting or promoting personal interests. | Sensory injection, thought realignment. |
| 11. Referral aversives | Emotionally uncomfortable asking existing clients and contacts for the names of referrals. | Threat desensitization, yellow dot, sensory injection, thought zapping. |

behaviors of each type of call-reluctant sales professional and the best corrective techniques to apply.

## Multiple Types, Multiple Cures

Based on our research with call-reluctant salespeople and sales managers, there is genuine cause for optimism. Most cases of authentic call reluctance can be corrected or at least substantially improved. But more than one corrective technique is needed to accomplish that end. What works for one type doesn't necessarily work for others. In fact, applying the wrong procedure typically makes matters worse than if nothing were done at all.

One technique, *thought zapping,* works for certain types of call reluctance by interrupting negative behaviors in progress. Threat desensitization is used to gradually reduce the intensity of the fear response in certain call-reluctant types (doomsayers, for example). Negative image projection attacks the escape and avoidance patterns found in certain forms of call reluctance as if they were addictions. Fear inversion is specifically designed for hyperpros. The yellow dot technique is effective for teaching people with certain types of call reluctance how to transfer the relaxation response to anxiety-provoking targets like the telephone. Sensory injection floods the nervous system with cues to relax before benign cues in the prospecting environment can signal it to become distressed. There are other techniques. The key is not so much the technique as it is the match with the forms of call reluctance most likely to be responsive and the order in which the techniques are applied.

Which type of call reluctance is most common among sales professionals in general? (See Table 3.2.) Most people think it's stage fright—the fear of speaking before groups of prospective buyers.

On the surface, that makes sense. Most people identify fear of speaking before groups as the most common fear among

Table 3.2 The Most Frequent Types of Call Reluctance.

| Type | Rank |
| --- | --- |
| Yielders | 1 (most frequent) |
| Overpreparers | 2 |
| Emotionally unemancipated | 3 |
| Separationists | 4 |
| Hyperpros | 5 |
| Role accepters | 6 |
| Socially self-conscious | 7 |
| Stage fright sufferers | 8 |
| Telephobics | 9 |
| Referral aversives | 10 |
| Doomsayers | 11 (least frequent) |

non-sales professionals. It's not. Yielders, who fear being considered pushy or intrusive, are the most common type of call-reluctant salespeople. Which type is the least common? Doomsayers. It's relatively rare to find a doomsayers in sales. Most doom-sayers abandon contact-dependent careers in favor of more procedural or analytical opportunities in administration, data processing, or the hard sciences.

## Industry Profiles

Call-reluctance profiles vary according to industry. Each industry has its own call-reluctance signature—the tendency of sales professionals in that industry to have a predominant type of call reluctance.

Since the early 1980s, psychologists have been conducting comparative research with sales professionals across a variety of industries. To acquire desired measures, they designed a specialized test to detect call reluctance and its impostors. It provided a

great deal of previously unknown information about how call reluctance works in various industries, and it recorded for the first
time the actual impact that call-reluctance attitudes have on sales
performance dollars. Like any breakthrough, it shed some light
and created some heat. Call reluctance, the missing link in the
sales performance equation, could now be measured.

Researchers found that stockbrokers tend to struggle with
call reluctance more than any other group of direct sales professionals. Brokers become wary of prospecting because they dread
(actually, they pre-experience) being humiliated by prospective
buyers who may question their professional integrity or doubt
their technical competence. So, many brokers prospect with hesitation. Does it matter? In 1985, experienced brokers with call-
reluctant attitudes produced an average of only $40,000 of
commissions. Those without call-reluctant attitudes produced almost $170,000 during the same period.

"Financial planners are not call-reluctant. They are professionals who don't have to prospect or self-promote." That's what the
editor of one of the financial planning industry's trade publications said. That's not, however, what researchers found. Financial
planners tend to have toxic levels of hyperpro call reluctance that
is characterized by vigorously denying the presence of prospecting
problems and piously insisting that prospecting is vulgar and un-
becoming. Because conventional prospecting is both unacceptable
and unnecessary in that profession, researchers can only speculate
on the number of financial planners who, at this very moment, are
sitting alone in their offices waiting for prospective clients to call
on them.

According to data, office equipment sales professionals
are making calls. Unfortunately, because of their social self-
consciousness, many of them are calling on the wrong people.
They're making potent presentations to non-decision makers.

Data-processing sales professionals are disposed to elevated
levels of overpreparer call reluctance, which is characterized by

putting more time and effort into preparing to make sales calls than into actually making them. This form of call reluctance is often found in people who have strong technical interests (systems engineers, systems analysts, programmers, and so on). Finding call reluctance in data-processing sales professionals was not altogether unexpected because many of them came from procedural or technical backgrounds. Given their predispositions, when this form of call reluctance is neglected, it can become devastating. Entire sales organizations can be enchanted into suspended animation by the rapture of endless streams of technical trivia. As an example, not too long ago, a company was considering buying some additional computer systems. In response to advertising, company representatives went to a large retail outlet of a very well known company. The facilities were warm and inviting. But, to their surprise, none of the sales professionals got up from the microcomputers they were pecking on. They just glanced up and went back to their pittering. The company representatives felt uncertain. Were they customers or annoyances? Apparently, in that store, they are the same thing. After conspicuously loitering for awhile, they left. They had computers to buy. The store lost a large sale.

Insurance agents, as a group, tend to suffer from role acceptance—an unexpressed, unresolved sense of guilt and shame centered on their career choice. The cavalier behavior and forced positive attitudes the public tends to incorrectly associate with all insurance agents are actually just compensations used by call-reluctant agents to keep the negative feelings they are struggling with at a safe distance.

As a group, radio and television airtime sales professionals appear to have minimal call reluctance. Data are presently being gathered on sales professionals in the industrial chemical industry. Automobile salespeople are currently being studied as well. As expected, sales professionals in seminar or "party" sales settings must be able to function effectively in front of groups. Yet, because of major gaps in the systems used to select and train them, an unusually high percentage of motivated, goal-driven people in this profession fail because they are emotionally unable to prospect or sell to groups!

## Age, Sex, and Call Reluctance

Technical research has also shown that women in direct sales are not significantly more—or less—prone to call reluctance than their male counterparts. Women in only two call-reluctance categories tend to suffer slightly more than men: emotionally unemancipated (calling on family members) and stage fright sufferers. But even for those two types, the differences are insignificant.

What about age and experience? Call reluctance does appear to be influenced by age. Though the pattern is complex, the total amount of call reluctance tends to increase with age. Among other things, this suggests that sales veterans should not consider themselves out of harm's way regarding call reluctance. Recent studies conducted with certain sales groups, however, have shown a stronger relationship with the amount of sales experience: Call reluctance increases as experience increases. If this is confirmed by repeated studies, it would reduce the importance of age and would provide additional support for the argument that several forms of call reluctance are actually acquired from sales managers and from the sales training environment.

Call reluctance norms now exist for many sales cultures. New studies are completed each month as international awareness and interest in the subject increase.

# Chapter 4

# Reaching the Next Level

Many sales professionals reach a comfort level with their sales production, but that level is far below their potential for success. In the financial services industry, only those sales professionals who reach the next level accomplish MDRT status. Here are some of the ways they boost their sales and income.

Regardless of how long you have been in the business of sales or how successful you have been, you may discover that moving off the production plateau you have reached is a difficult task. Ultimately, sales professionals decide for themselves whether they are on or have been on a plateau; however, there are two quick ways to make that determination:

1. If you feel a sense of frustration because you know that you have more ability and more talents than you are using.

2. If your production is failing to increase at the minimum level of between 25 percent and 30 percent per year.

If you can't seem to achieve that minimum increase (an objective measurement), or if you feel, in spite of a good performance "on paper," that you are producing at less than your potential (a subjective measurement), then, in all probability, you are on a production plateau.

Sales and production plateaus appear to be the result of a failure to identify and terminate one or more irrational fears—fears that can motivate you to actually sabotage yourself and your well-thought-out plans and objectives. As an example, suppose you have made a commitment to ask five centers of influence per week to give you the names of five referred leads. In most weeks, you never seem to find the time to call all five centers. When you do make a call or two, and compile a short list of prospects, you feel that you might be imposing on a friendship, or you experience so much self-consciousness or anxiety that you either abandon the idea or decide to ask at another time. Your irrational fears are, in essence, sabotaging yourself and your future.

Have you found yourself procrastinating from time to time? How often have you decided to get organized and then, within days, found that you are disorganized again? How often have you gone on a diet and been unable to stick with it? How often do you sleep six hours or more per night? How often have you felt discouraged, frustrated, anxious, depressed, or angry during the past 60 days? How often do you have to have a drink or two at lunch? Do you get back spasms? Headaches? Skin or rash problems? Asthma? Ulcers? High blood pressure?

If you responded "yes" to any of these questions (there are many more), then you are fighting yourself and you may be losing. You are sabotaging yourself and your future. Your inability to eliminate these symptoms will do more than freeze you on a sales plateau. It will narrow and confine your life in general and your sales career in particular. To eliminate these problems, it is first necessary to understand three important facts.

### 1.  You are not alone.

Almost everyone you will ever come in contact with is living far below his or her potential and is experiencing feelings of frustration because of a deep awareness of that personal shortfall. William James suggested that human beings use only between 10 and 12 percent of their potential. If that estimate is true, then perhaps you should multiply your production by a number as high as 10, to determine your potential for the coming year.

The problem is that it is easier to talk about reaching full potential than it is to make the necessary changes. Few people even know where to start. Many begin by developing plans and establishing goals; others find their start in educational classes. Neither choice is a poor way to begin improving, but both are off-target for the majority. A preponderance of evidence suggests that the principal reason for failure to live up to personal potential is the presence of one or more irrational fears, which is a psychological issue.

### 2.  *It is never too late to change.*

Regardless of how long you have carefully nurtured your problem or how old you are today, you can confront and defeat that problem. For most people, thirty-year-old problems can be permanently terminated in six to eight weeks.

### 3.  *You can begin changing today.*

By using proven behavior-modification techniques, you can make change happen immediately.

Let's look at the first step in the change process: identification of a change target. Give at least one response to the following question (a list of responses is all right too):

> If you were going to improve the one single activity that would produce the most significant results in your life, what would that activity be?

As a sales professional, your progression up the achievement or success ladder seems to follow a fairly logical process. Initially, you are introduced to sales-skill training. You are taught how to approach strangers, present solutions, and close a sale. Your sales training includes developing approaches, answering objections, and motivating the prospect to purchase your products and services. In addition to those basic sales skills, you are introduced to annual goals and you develop daily work plans and a reasonable set of priorities. All of this training is useful and necessary.

More advanced sales-skill training can introduce you to some powerful techniques for disarming anger, probing the emotions of a prospect, accurately perceiving the prospect, and sending and receiving correct nonverbal messages. These behavioral techniques regarding perception, persuasion, and assertion training have been developed in psychology laboratories.

The second area of development, or the next progressive step that sales professionals take, is technical training. Most salespeople improve their sales effectiveness as they increase their understanding of the products and services they sell. Not only is there an immediate growth in the individual's success, but a secondary and perhaps even more meaningful impact occurs when the individual begins to realize: "I really am qualified to help people meet their needs."

The third developmental area is psychological training. How often have you found yourself subject to unidentifiable anxieties, fears, frustrations, and angers, as well as feelings of worthlessness and depression? Do you deny them, as a way to avoid accepting responsibility for yourself and for your actions? Instead, you have to face them. They are the critical issues that put you on a plateau, and they will have to be defeated if you are going to make a significant and permanent leap off that plateau.

When we discuss the sales and technical aspects of our business, we are articulate and sure of ourselves. There is little to dispute in a discussion of how many direct-mail pieces should be mailed out and received back, or how many doors you have to knock on to make an appointment, or how many preapproach letters must be sent before you are granted one appointment. However, when discussing matters of personality, behavior, and emotions, articulateness vanishes and we become unsure of our positions. And there seems little doubt that this developmental area, which offers the least amount of information, is directly in control of the other two.

For example, if you have a fear of rejection, teaching you a new cold-canvass door opener will not help you knock on any more doors. Your problem is rejection, and until you confront and defeat that problem, you are only wasting your time and effort. You will continue to experience frustration and to wonder why you are unable to use all of the new super sales-training materials. If you have a deep-rooted fear of success, introducing you to more advanced concepts will not create additional sales. Your fear of success will paralyze your desire to prospect and sell.

The central question becomes: Who is addressing the psychological training issue? Buzzing around it is a cluster of other questions: Where do you go? What do you do? Is it effective? Is it expensive? How long does it take? If I talk to a shrink, does that mean that there is something the matter with me?

There is more and more evidence that individuals who want to make quantum leaps in their effectiveness, their production, and their personal lives will find the source of that leap in psychological training. Hundreds of psychologists around the country are now using behavior modification techniques to improve the quality of people's lives. Few—if any—professional sports teams are *not* using behavioral scientists, and industries are slowly discovering that the best source of new production is the development and improvement of their own people.

During the past fifteen years, psychologists have been untangling all sorts of complicating issues—they now dry out alcoholics, toilet-train youngsters in half a day, turn delinquents into scholars in a semester, and focus on high-achieving salespeople and train them to make changes that will produce gigantic increases in their production.

For example, one group of stockbrokers who had earned a minimum of $100,000 in a one-year period were introduced to a behavior modification program in January of the new year. During the first four months, their *average* increase in dollar income was 285 percent. Within the group, some specific increases far exceeded the average. One-fourth of the group earned more money during the first quarter of the new year than they did in the entire previous year. No one increased at a ratio of less than 30 percent. Interestingly, the group's effort was focused directly on the development of new accounts, and the income developed from the new accounts averaged 63 percent of their business. Perhaps even more surprising, this group had experienced a deficit of new accounts during the previous three years.

No technology is as useful to you personally as the one that can teach you how to modify and control your own behavior, your personal feelings, and your intimate thoughts. Today's behavior modification techniques offer choices for making positive permanent changes in your behavior. You *can* move off your personal plateau and improve the quality of your life.

Let's discuss the reasons for your problems and why they can glue you to your production plateau. More often than not, the roots of problems are hidden in irrational fears. The word "irrational" is used because there is literally no reason or explanation why you should fear any of these situations; yet you do. The basic tenet of behavior modification theory is that you do, think, and feel as a direct result of previous learning experiences; that is, you actually *learned* how to fear rejection, just as you learned to fear snakes and death. Benefits are being realized from behavior modification because when people are able to understand all of their behavior—as well as their feelings and thoughts—in terms of learning theory, it is possible to teach them how to "unlearn" negative or self-destructive behaviors and how to "learn" positive or self-enhancing patterns of behavior that will introduce new feelings and new thoughts.

## Living with Fears

Perhaps the most common and most ridiculous thought that opens a floodgate of fears is: "I have to be perfect" or "I have to win all of the time, and every loss is a catastrophe."

Everyone has irrational fears; however, not everyone has the same collection. Fears become quite specific. One MDRT sales associate was fearless during every step of an interview until it was time to ask for a referred lead. His specific fear of rejection was centered around asking for a referral, and that was the only time he was aware of any anxiety. He was succeeding quite well, but he had a psychological problem—and psychological problems require psychological solutions. This sales professional worked with a psychologist for five weeks. By focusing directly on his problem and using some specific change strategies, he terminated the problem. The following year, his sales almost doubled! Not bad for a guy who was stuck on one production level for four years.

Typically, sales professionals learn to live with their fears. They develop prospecting and sales systems that make it possible for them to exist but not to reach their potential. Sales professionals who are stuck on plateaus often begin to justify themselves and their position to everyone with whom they come in contact. They can give you a dozen reasons why they are better off where they are rather than where they would be if they improved. One big hitter explained in great detail why he was better off producing $5 million in sales per year than he would be if he produced $10 million or $20 million. He further stated that people who produced more than he did were absolutely crazy because they would end up earning less than he did. For example, they not only had to hire an administrative assistant, but they had to worry about employee work habits.

Generally, irrational fears are beyond a person's voluntary control, and the individual may or may not be able to recognize the problem. Even if you can recognize your fear, you may lack the ability to describe it or to develop a program that will effectively correct it. Typically, you continue to grope for solutions, and you try goal setting, motivation, and pep talks—all to no avail. Intellectually, you may understand that you are dealing with a problem that is actually causing you to sabotage yourself. You may even tell yourself, "I shouldn't be afraid of making cold calls," but you are unable to reduce the anxiety associated with the activity, and you experience a very high level of psychological pain. At that point, the normal response is to escape the pain and to resolve never to come in contact with that pain again. You then develop the symptoms that are your barriers to avoid the fear. You rely on them because they work. They reduce the anxiety or the psychological pain.

For example, you might learn: "If I procrastinate long enough, I will not have enough time to follow up on these phone calls." And, at the end of the day, you are right; you *don't* have enough time to make the calls, so you commit yourself to making the calls tomorrow—or some other day.

*What techniques do you use to avoid doing things that you know you should be doing?* Or, from a different slant: *What techniques do you use to continue doing those activities that you know you should not be doing?* The basic responses to all fears are the various behaviors that an individual uses to avoid an object of fear or anxiety in any manner possible when confronted with a choice. Anxiety serves a purpose; it tells you when you are in danger. Whether the danger is real or imagined, your thinking narrows and begins to look for immediate escape routes. This is when "Igor"—the name we'll use to identify your primitive nervous system—steps in.

Igor is so primitive that he lacks the ability to reason or use logic. He reacts when he feels threatened. He creates anxiety and panic. All he wants to do is escape and not have to deal with the problem. Igor short-circuits any thinking process. He blocks out headaches, back pains, and even sales appointments, and he runs away as fast as he can. Later, he may realize how silly it was to act in that manner. But, at the time, Igor's only concern was psychological safety. He generated so much anxiety that his only thought was: "How the hell can I get out of here?"

Some people are controlled by this level of masked fear. Fear-driven sales professionals realize it, but their anxieties unfortunately make them unable to move off their production plateaus. From time to time, everyone falls into a rut; the problem gets magnified when a person stays in the rut.

Rather than discuss all of the irrational fears that people suffer from, let's introduce a few of the more common ones that sales professionals must confront and defeat.

The fear of:

- ✓ Looking foolish.
- ✓ Rejection.
- ✓ Being "found out."
- ✓ Making an incorrect decision.
- ✓ Failing.
- ✓ Being too successful.
- ✓ Being wrong.

## Fear of Looking Foolish

The very thought of doing something that others may think is ridiculous fills you with fear. You are so fearful of doing something that you will later regret (you are generally your own severest critic) that, because *anything* you may say or do carries the risk of looking foolish to *someone,* you avoid activities more and more, and your inhibitions grow. Because areas of spontaneity and creativity are too dangerous to risk, you become a spectator rather than a participator.

Closely linked to this fear is the fear of being wrong (described later), which follows a similar pattern but has consequences that are usually less devastating. Not one sales professional would deliberately choose to look foolish or wrong, but most of them will risk it and retain their spontaneity. The problem occurs when the fear of being wrong or looking foolish takes over.

## Fear of Rejection

This fear of being disliked by some people can cause you to placate people at the expense of your own goals and self-respect. It sensitizes you to other persons. Even a fleeting facial expression of dissatisfaction signals potential rejection. You interpret any disagreement or disappointment with another person as a rejection. Every rejection represents an overwhelming catastrophe, and you can't cope with it.

## Fear of Being "Found Out"

You think that if people "really know" you, if you are exposed for what you "really are," they will reject you. Many times, you can't even be sure what qualities would be "exposed." However, some fears can be quite specific, such as: "They will find out that I do not know what I am talking about." Even if you are guilty of these things to some extent, it's not the cause of your fear. Fears are not that reasonable.

## Fear of Making an Incorrect Decision

You've met people who ponder every decision, no matter how small. They weigh each alternative and discuss it with as many people as possible, and then justify their long decision making by explaining that it always helps to get someone else's opinion. Indecision portrays a lack of confidence, not a concern for the prospect (as the indecisive person will rationalize). Statements such as "I only want to do what is best for my client" fail when the real problem is more closely tied to your lack of self-esteem, reflected in your fear of making an incorrect decision.

Igor demonstrates his control when he creates anxiety and stimulates self-doubts. Igor's goal is to avoid the anxiety by avoiding the problem. If you become so anxious that you cannot make a decision, you are relieved of the responsibility by experiencing migraine headaches. (It's almost impossible to make decisions when you suffer from migraines.) Here's a case history of a sales professional. William achieved enormous success under normal circumstances. He grew up in Newport Beach, California, and graduated from the University of Southern California. During his career, he developed clients in population centers two hundred miles away. William was articulate, decisive, assertive, perceptive, and spontaneous. After some years in the business, he began to make incorrect decisions. He failed to follow his own best judgment, and he procrastinated when given even the simplest tasks. His bad decisions soon compounded his problems. He began to lose his self-confidence, and his self-esteem hit rock bottom. The worst part of the whole situation was that he could not foresee the situation getting any better. The need to make prospecting decisions traumatized him, and he decided to leave the business. Those who met William at the bottom of his long slide out of the business saw two realities: (1) he had sufficient sales and technical skills to be a great success in sales, and (2) he had been severely shaken when one negative experience piled on the back of another one. William began working in a self-administered behavior modification program designed to help him identify the source of his problems. (That task is more difficult than it may sound. According to research sources, sales professionals typically model 8,000 possible behaviors.) After identifying the problem, William used a specific change format to confront and defeat the self-destructive pattern or behavior. Within a period of twelve weeks, William had solved his problem and reacquired his self-confidence, and he was producing business—big business.

## Fear of Being Wrong

One of our greatest fears is the fear of being wrong and then being found out (and embarrassed). It is tied to our fear of being inadequate. An individual who can admit an error or accept responsibility for an error has a strong sense of personal identity. This is part of succeeding and being decisive. Those who have low self-esteem go to great lengths to prove ridiculous points. They rely on very aggressive maneuvers to support their views, even to the point of destroying a relationship. Their need to protect their self-worth from all threats overpowers every rational thought. Typically, they "repent" later and apologize. When their apology fails to put the former relationship back together again, they are somewhat astounded.

These people are easily angered, and they excuse themselves (they think) by saying, "I have a bad temper." They may end an argument by shouting, "I know what I am talking about, so stop arguing with me." Generally, the anger reflects a lack of social skills and a fear that they may be discovered as being wrong. Many people report that they know sales professionals who have never been able to admit that they made an error or that their judgment may have been incorrect. Rather than bolstering their self-esteem or the esteem garnered from other people, their I-am-always-right tack works in reverse. Other people wonder why they overreact and are afraid to examine anything with an unbiased mindset.

## Fear of Failing

Perfectionism is the mirror image of a strong fear of failure. Certain professions require more perfectionism than others. For example, all pilots and all surgeons should strive to be perfect in their work responsibilities. But when perfectionism is carried into the sales profession, it is disastrous. You must not expect to be perfect. Generalized perfectionism is often the result of over-compensating for feelings of weakness or of inadequacy, derived from parents or superiors who taught that winning was everything. Fearing judgment, children react by striving to please and trying to reach even the most impossible of goals . . . perfection.

One of the most pervasive aspects of this fear is that you will not only fail to be perfect, but you will find it almost impossible to force yourself to do things at which you do not feel competent. More and more, you will tend to become a spectator rather than a participant. Instead of learning new techniques, you will tend to put new concepts down. Your logic (as irrational as it may be) will tell you that if new information is made to appear invalid, then you will not have to go through the pain of learning something new (and feeling imperfect during the process).

## Fear of Being Too Successful

Recently, a forty-three-year-old MDRT sales associate said, "Me? Afraid of being successful? You have got to be kidding! Everything I do is directed toward succeeding. I set goals, develop activity plans, make positive affirmations, and have even tried hypnosis." This sales professional was succeeding in the business, yet he was unhappy, frustrated, uneasy, uncertain about the future, and the host of a small ulcer.

One of the principal reasons why so many sales professionals have been sitting on plateaus is: They have a deep-seated fear of being too successful. That fear is so universal that almost every sales professional has it to some degree. It does not inhibit use of some talents, but it certainly interferes with use of all talents.

For example, it is not uncommon for sales professionals who are exceeding their companies' targets for sales to develop a sickness that makes it impossible for them to work. Or, they may announce an uncontrollable desire to take a few weeks off to attend some personal event—even if the reward for winning the competition is a trip abroad. As soon as they discover they are leading the contest, they begin to experience anxiety, and Igor begins to offer solutions that are self-destructive. An interesting aspect of this subtle intervention by Igor is that he offers solutions that seem to make sense at the time. Only in retrospect do we see the flaws in the argument. Was there really a need to attend the personal event? (You chose to miss all the previous ones.) Or: You deserve a few weeks off, contest or no contest. After all, if you do not get some immediate rest, you may develop a serious illness.

The fear of success can be defined as an unconscious fear of what one considers to be important and desirable. To understand the fear of success, it is necessary to consider this aspect of your personality in connection with two adjacent variables—the fear of failing and the wish to succeed. The fear of failure may be defined as a conscious fear that a person's incompetence will result in specific mistakes. The wish to succeed may be defined as a person's conscious drive for effective accomplishment of a specific objective. The fear of success may be defined as the individual's unconscious fear that the success is not justified.

Typically, an individual who fears success establishes goals, develops plans for achieving them, and then begins actively pursuing them with full resources and energies. But when the goal is within reach, anxiety surfaces. The individual begins to rationalize his or her position and concludes that the goal is not really desired. New goals are developed, and the net result is a cycle in which rationalizations crop up. People who fear success and find themselves on this treadmill may echo Woody Allen's line in his movie, *Annie Hall,* when he quoted Groucho Marx: "I would not want to belong to a club that would have me as a member."

The fear of success threatens the individual. As long as that fear is at an unconscious level, it is even more destructive because it is impossible to modify a behavior that is hidden. Once the problem is identified, however, it can be successfully confronted and defeated.

The important difference between the fear of success and the fear of failure is that the former is seldom recognized. Some people fear future achievement; others fear the success they already have achieved. Consider the individual who says, "I don't want to be number one; number two is just fine. I'm lazy and I don't want to continue proving myself year after year. I like the recognition, but I don't want the responsibility." To this person, the danger of being prominent is equal to the danger of responsibility.

Another variation appears in this particular syndrome—the sales professional who makes sure he or she never reaches the top. This individual prefers to stay on a plateau, where it is safe.

To determine whether you are on a production plateau as a result of one or more of the fears mentioned above, identify the reasons for your frustrations. Do you believe that you can be a much better sales professional, but your fears are holding you back? Examine your production levels over the past three years. If your growth rate is less than 20 percent, you are on a plateau. The first step in moving off a plateau is to admit you are on one. Begin your action plan of analyzing your fears and terminating the behaviors that keep you from being successful.

## The Fear Process

If fears can be unlearned, why do unreasonable fears linger on in real-life situations, especially when the individual wants to change? This question has a two-part answer.

First, each person learns fears that, however irrational, are powerful enough to control his or her behavior. An easy, but destructive, way to reduce fear is to avoid the situation (feel too sick to work) or escape the feared situation (procrastination). Each time a sales professional uses avoidance techniques, his or her immediate anxiety decreases. However, the fear is being allowed to gain additional power each time the person reinforces the avoidance pattern. A spiral actually develops and pulls the person down. Being fearful, he or she avoids the activity that reinforces the fear, which creates more fear and makes the person want to avoid the activity even more.

Second, many people have misconceptions about the nature of change and the intentions of psychological intervention. They think that the purpose of therapy is to talk about, rather than devise, an active way to solve problems. Behavior modification focuses on an "action-change method."

Many people block their own progress in the presence of several conditions, including:

1. Failure to identify the root of the problem (the irrational fear of self-destructive behavior.

2. Refusal to accept personal responsibility for the problem.

3. Refusal to accept the possibility of personal change.

4. Lack of motivation to change.

5. Unwillingness to work at changing.

There are several myths about change, such as:

1. If people do not totally understand why they are the way they are, or why they feel the way they do, then they cannot change. (It is not necessary to unravel every aspect of a person's personality in order to change.)

2. People must understand all the reasons behind events in their formative years or they cannot change.

3. Change that occurs quickly is superficial.

4. Change requires years of therapy.

5. The internal message, "This is just the way I am."

## Behavior Change Alternatives

People have several alternatives when they become aware that they may be sabotaging themselves and their potential for additional production. They can ignore the negative behaviors and hope that they will go away by themselves—something that is not likely to happen. Or, they can hope to change negative behaviors by using "will power." This is often recommended because "Do It Yourself" is an American rule of life. The problem is that do-it-yourself therapy is foolhardy. The costs and chances for failing are too high.

# Behavior Modification

Behavior modification offers an effective alternative to do-it-yourself methods. Its techniques have been proven; its results are fast and permanent. The format requires first reducing or controlling anxiety and then applying the appropriate techniques to relearn how to act, think, and feel in self-enhancing ways.

There are four significant steps in the behavior modification change process. We can use the acronym **D E A R** to explain them:

**D** stands for **discovering** what your problems are and why you continue to respond to certain situations in a fearful manner.

**E** stands for **educating** yourself: How did you develop the fear, what triggers it, what are its antecedents, what does it cost to maintain it, and what payoffs do you receive by maintaining it?

**A** stands for **activities** of the program, which, if followed, will help you succeed in your change program.

**R** stands for **reinforcement.** Each successful experience will reinforce your ability to succeed in your change program.

## Thought Stopping

You can be either the victim or the beneficiary of your thoughts. Your thoughts can produce a self-fulfilling prophecy that will create or reduce anxiety. You might think or say to yourself: "If I talk to a certain prospect, he or she may ask me questions that I cannot answer, and I will look foolish or feel like a peddler." When you think thoughts like these, you increase the likelihood that the situation will occur. When you feel anxiety because of your negative thinking, you can stop it by "stopping" your thoughts. The goal of thought stopping is to break the habit of fear-inducing anticipatory thoughts. There are two rules for thought stopping: (1) Do it as soon as possible, and (2) do it every time your anticipatory thoughts start to occur. When these thoughts gain momentum, they become harder to stop.

## Thought Switching

When you think, daydream, or fantasize, you are instructing yourself to behave in a particular manner—often, a fearful one—and these instructions become habits. One way to change a negative or self-destructive habit is to establish a powerful self-enhancing one. This technique, called thought switching, is designed to establish and issue positive statements that help you replace fear-inducing self-instructions with competent self-instructions that eventually replace the negative or anxious thoughts.

The key benefit of thought switching is that it actually helps you turn off your anxiety-producing thoughts and replaces them with thoughts of something else. When that occurs, your anxiety dissipates and you are then able to increase your activity. The increased activity will reinforce the new behaviors and, before long, you will have "learned" how to act in a new and positive way.

## Success Rehearsal

In a success rehearsal, you practice handling your fears by imagining scenes in which you cope successfully with your fears. You imagine yourself being overwhelmed by your anticipatory anxiety and then overcoming it. In devising your scenes, make sure they represent situations you can expect yourself to handle with little practice. If the imagery is too far ahead of you, you'll think it's impossible and give up. A positive consequence must always conclude your rehearsals; you must succeed.

## Internal Dialogue Control

When you perceive yourself to be anxious, you may wonder whether you are going to "lose control" and stand by helplessly as your feelings of tension increase. That doesn't have to happen. You can take a more active and direct approach to coping with the thoughts that accompany anxiety by controlling what you say to yourself. Begin to conduct sessions of positive self-dialogue. Talk to yourself aloud. Your learning will be more effective if you can hear the tone and inflections of your voice. You might say: "There's no point in getting upset. In a moment, I'll be fine. Relax, just relax; I can handle this call."

You can practice your self- (or internal) dialogue in a private spot in your home, as you walk around the block or the exercise track, or while driving to your office. The important thing is to *do it when you begin to feel anxious.* If your anxiety begins to overcome you in a setting where it isn't feasible to talk aloud to yourself, take a break and find a private place to go over your self-dialogue again.

There is an increasing awareness among psychotherapists that behavior modification offers a proven approach to treating self-sabotaging ways of thinking, feeling, and acting. Literally thousands of research studies, ranging from case studies to sophisticated controlled experiments, have shown behavioral therapy techniques to be successful in helping people resolve problem responses.

Behavior therapy is a collection of techniques using therapeutic tools. It is not a new religion or philosophy of life. It is a positive way to help people eliminate fears and behaviors that can stop them from being everything they can be.

Salespeople who choose to use behavior modification techniques no longer have to sit back passively, ignoring anxieties and fears or waiting for them to go away. They can look squarely at undesired habits as problems that can be eliminated. By directing and changing their behavior, salespeople can remove obstacles to their own success.

## Relearning Through Behavior Modification

Behavior modification is based on the concept that you can be trained, through a relearning process, to overcome both your irrational fears and the symptoms that you have developed to fight those fears. Fear is learned, and you master "unlearning" it through the strategies outlined in behavioral psychology. The first step is to identify your fear. You then develop a specific change program that provides you with individual and specific feedback so you can fine-tune the behavior change techniques to suit your specific personality.

The method of reducing your phobias is based on three assumptions, each of which is supported by many years of research and development by outstanding behavioral scientists who studied thousands of individuals:

1. You can change.

2. The change you affect will be permanent.

3. The effort needed to change can only come from you.

Think about the first basic assumption: You can change. Too often, people fail to accept personal responsibility for their individual behaviors, thoughts, and feelings. They truly believe that the way they are today is the way they will always be. They sentence themselves to a life of mediocrity with statements such as: "If God didn't want me this way, He wouldn't have made me this way," or "I don't have what it takes to be a big hitter," or "I don't think I really can change."

Change is not only possible, it is probable. Have you ever observed or known a person who would stay with a bad situation when a better offer came along? Change is the better offer that you make to yourself.

The second assumption is that the change you bring about will be permanent. Change can begin to occur within six to eight weeks. It is not necessary to devote years to a change program. Some people change within a period of a few days, and others take as long as fourteen weeks, but most people change in six to eight weeks.

Individuals who terminate a problem discover that the change is permanent. The termination requires a planned, predetermined process which, although it is intense, is not impossible.

One study involved three hundred sales professionals. Their efforts to overcome serious problems were followed for thirty-five months. These were the results:

1. Seventy-two percent reported a complete and permanent termination of the problem.

2. Seventeen percent reported a change, but not a complete elimination of the problem. (For example: "I do not experience as much anxiety when I ask for a referral, but I still experience some anxiety.")

3. Seven percent reported no change.

4. Four percent did not respond to follow-up questionnaires.

The researchers indicated that the second and third groups needed a longer change format.

The third assumption is that you, and only you, can terminate irrational fears, through practice and effort. Fear termination training is an active process. Wishing, thinking, or hoping you will change will be ineffective. Listening to a lecture will produce little or no change in your behavior. You need to actively follow a well-designed change program and practice the change technique every day.

Remember, you are not alone. It is never too late to change, and you can begin today. Some people spend their lives living far below their potential. Don't be one of them.

## A Plan for Self-Improvement

Do you doubt that your personality can be improved? If so, read how a sales professional in Boston cited his own life as an example of how people can almost entirely change their personality:

> I grew up the son of a minister, and had to sit in the front seat during all church services, and in sessions like prayer meeting on Wednesday evening I had a tendency to sneak into the back seat, taking no part in the proceedings. A preacher's son is often singled out in the community and made fun of by other boys. The combination of all this resulted in a substantial inferiority complex and a fear and dislike of meeting people.

The summer that I was 20 years old I got a job as a book sales professional and for some time did joint work with an experienced book sales professional. He taught me exactly what to say and drilled me and drilled me in how to say it, so that I got to the point where I looked forward to going to the various boarding houses, where my teacher-prospects lived while attending summer normal school, to attempt to interest them in buying a set of books.

Knowing exactly what to say and how to say it, I got so that I lost all fear of meeting people, and my wife, who knew me before and after this experience, is an authority for the statement that I got to talking so freely that I have never stopped since.

Others, including many of the contributors to this book, can vouch for this sales professional's social ease, poise, and likableness.

## Learn to Feel Your Words

A Canadian MDRT sales professional told how he had quit school rather early in life and thus lacked a formal education. Realizing the importance of effectiveness in speech when one hoped to earn a living by talking, he put forward a plan of action. "I decided," he says, "that it was imperative that I learn to talk effectively—learn to say words as though I really felt them. As one means of developing this, I grasped every opportunity to make a public speech because it helped me to formulate my thoughts in an organized way and gave me poise and speech practice in the process of delivery. I count this as one of the most important things I ever did."

So impressed is this sales professional with the value of his experience that when he is looking for college students to join his company, he is much less interested in athletes than in those who have been active in debating, dramatics, and other extracurricular activities that demand practice in speaking.

## Develop Poise and Assurance

Another example of the value of public speaking is contained in the narrative of a 35-year-old sales professional, after one year in the business. He was shy when he was in the presence of more than one prospect, so he decided to take a public speaking course to develop more poise and assurance. He went through the usual period of embarrassment and the hemming-and-hawing stage, but now is considered by his former teacher as one of his best pupils. The sales professional got himself invited to speak at a small-town men's club fifteen miles away. He wrote out a talk, memorized every word, and drove northward on the appointed day. It went better than he thought; it always does. Now he only uses notes and is pretty cocky about speaking. He says, "It brought me out tremendously and greatly improved my assurance and presence when with people."

Another sales professional tells an interesting story about a member of his public speaking class who, for the first ten or so lessons, could scarcely get through one sentence before an audience. The perspiration literally had to be mopped from his face. Gradually, he developed poise. The next year, he was elected president of his class. He used to hesitate and even blushed in personal contacts. He was so transformed, we are told, that except for his features, one would never suspect that he was the same man.

## Do a Self-Check

Many traits make up a good personality. A list of such traits is shown in Table 4.1. As was suggested earlier, self-analysis is useful in determining faults and focusing attention on them. The next process, however, requires practice in association with people, not more analysis and introspection.

| Table 4.1 Self-Analysis. | | | | | | |
|---|---|---|---|---|---|---|
| Name _____ | Date _____ | Rating: | 1 | 2 | 3 | 4 5 |

Qualities:

| | |
|---|---|
| Ability to carry out my own plans | _____ |
| Ability to work steadily | _____ |
| Imagination—vision | _____ |
| Ambition | _____ |
| Self-confidence | _____ |
| Enthusiasm | _____ |
| Ability to influence people through their feelings | _____ |
| Poise | _____ |
| Ability to concentrate | _____ |
| Sincerity | _____ |
| Forcefulness | _____ |
| Ability to get other person's point of view | _____ |
| Good health | _____ |
| Loyalty | _____ |
| Ability to restrain my argumentativeness | _____ |
| Voice quality | _____ |
| Ability to put other people at their ease | _____ |
| Ability to dress well | _____ |
| Ability to become well known and favorably regarded | _____ |
| Cooperativeness | _____ |
| Memory | _____ |
| Courtesy | _____ |
| Sportsmanship | _____ |
| Sense of humor | _____ |
| Tact | _____ |
| Friendliness | _____ |
| Persistence | _____ |

As you are completing the self-analysis in Table 4.1, be aware that a similar plan was used by Benjamin Franklin over 200 years ago to improve his personality. Here are the steps:

1. Rate yourself on each of the traits, without egotism or inferiority: 1 and 2 = above average; 3 = average; 4 and 5 = below average.

2. Make a list of the 4s and 5s; then list any 3s that you believe should be added to your program of development.

3. Select only one or two entries on the list as the first one(s) to be attacked. Then assign yourself specific practical activities that you can perform every day in connection with your daily calls and your social contacts.

4. Continue this procedure for two weeks. Check yourself, and continue for another period until you note that the improvement level that you want is becoming habitual. Then add another trait or two that need attention.

5. At the end of six months, rate yourself again to measure the extent of your improvement.

With this process of self-analysis, you will quickly find that the very intangible problem of improving personality reduces itself to the improvement of a few definite traits. Your spouse, your manager, or someone else who is interested in your development can be of great help in this process. You may wish to make some extra copies and ask some of your family or friends to rate you on the various items.

Here are some examples of activities you can practice to improve certain traits:

1. Improving your memory for names. The cause of poor memory for names is lack of attention and repetition.

The remedy lies in building your own memory plan based on these exercises:

a. When introduced, be sure you understand the name clearly. If you do not, ask that it be repeated.

b. When you address the person in the ensuing conversation, repeat the name as often as possible without its being conspicuous.

c. Try to associate the name with something familiar to you.

d. At the end of the day, recall the names of everyone whom you met during the day. Write the names out and try to visualize each one.

2. Developing sociability or affability:

a. Force yourself to join organizations and activities that bring you in contact with others and require working closely with them. Consider joining the Chamber of Commerce, and let it be known that you would like to help. Consciously push yourself to meet people and make business contacts.

b. Put yourself in situations that call for cordiality and tact. In one company, a new sales professional who lacked affability was brought into the office and put at the gate, where he had the job of meeting and greeting all visitors. He was prompted on just what to say and how to say it even to the cultivating of a proper smile. He was given all sorts of jobs that required him to gain the cooperation of people. His manager kept him under constant observation, pointed out his lack of tact on occasions, and soon changed his whole manner of meeting people.

3. Developing a liking for people:

a. Every day, for the next week, make a list of the first ten people you meet. Opposite the name of each, write down one thing that you like about that person. Also make a list of all the people you dislike, and write down, alongside each name, all the favorable traits of the person that you can think of. A few weeks of doing these exercises will help you change your point of view until you begin to look for the good things in people and in life generally.

## The Most Valuable Hour Ever Spent

A manager who has given a great deal of attention to the improvement of personality reports the following sincere testimony from one of his sales professionals: "That hour in which we first went over my personal deficiencies was the most valuable hour I ever spent in my life. I was 28 years old and had never had an opportunity to go to a person who was interested and who could look at me in an impersonal fashion and help me size myself up."

Such an attitude is characteristic of all really ambitious, sincere sales professionals. They are interested in their personalities, and the more ambitious they are, the more willing they are to work on their own personal development. All sales professionals, no matter how successful they may be, can improve themselves if they will take the trouble to discover their weaknesses and then do the things that will help to overcome them.

## Can You Take It?

In his book, *Behaviorism* (Transaction Publisher, June 1998), John B. Watson puts it this way:

> Each man can watch his own way of acting and he will often be surprised when he comes to face the real stimuli that touch off his actions. Susceptibility to flattery, selfishness, avoiding difficult situations, unwillingness to show or to confess

weakness, inadequacy or lack of knowledge, jealousy, fear of rivals, fear of being made the scapegoat, hurling criticism upon others to escape it oneself—make up an unbelievable part of our natures.

The individual when he really faces himself is often almost (if not quite) overcome by what is revealed—infantile behavior, unethical standards—smothered over by the thinnest veneer of rationalization. Nakedness of "soul" can be faced only by the truly brave.

## Personality, Boiled Down

From the point of view of the prospect, you can probably reduce most of the desirable personality traits that we have discussed into four outstanding characteristics:

1. *Likableness.* The sales professional must be a person who is agreeable, friendly, and congenial. These characteristics have much to do with getting in to see prospects and getting names of prospects from friends and acquaintances.

2. *Forcefulness.* This trait is built on self-confidence and on a thorough knowledge of the business, but it also involves the manner of presenting the proposition. Forcefulness is largely a matter of physical energy and the proper use of the speaking voice.

3. *Zealousness.* The sales professional must have the right mental attitude toward his or her product or service, job responsibilities, and prospects. This attitude is a combination of enthusiasm and sincerity.

4. *Persistence.* This trait combines industry with determination. It is the quality that keeps a new sales professional from being turned away easily. It is also the quality that takes him or her back to see the prospect a second and third time.

These characteristics give great power to sales professionals who possess them in combination.

## Fifteen Ways to Boost Your Sales

Becoming accustomed to a growing economy is easy and dangerous. There are always pockets of problems, but sales professionals tend to forget that success is often more a function of a good economy than of their business acumen. If everyone else is doing well, the major challenge is how to pull ahead of the pack. Unfortunately, many sales professionals get a bit lazy, and that's when they can get caught short of their goals.

Here are fifteen ways to become more successful—to keep your business booming and give you the opportunity to gain a competitive advantage.

### 1. Develop a marketing plan.

"Seat-of-the-pants" marketing is neither fun nor rewarding. It's frustrating, confusing, counterproductive, and indicative of disorganization and of an inability to think through what needs to be accomplished. A useful marketing plan doesn't need to be a highly detailed document. It should be designed for implementing rather than for impressing management. A simple outline will do, if it covers the basic issues: audience, description, objective, message, expected results, schedule, and so forth.

What's on paper can always be changed or revised, but a written version helps the plan move forward on a consistent basis toward an agreed-on objective.

### 2. Select the right marketing tactics.

The business world is filled with nonsense thinking. Here are a few examples: "Direct mail doesn't work." (Tell this to PC Warehouse, L.L. Bean, and Victoria's Secret.) "Nobody reads ads." (Pass along this information to Microsoft, General

Motors, and Merck.) "Newsletters don't make sales." (Who said they did? Sales professionals are in charge of getting orders. Newsletters help create customers.) Selecting the medium that's most appropriate for a particular audience deserves serious attention and research. In most situations, the results of research can be related to creating a campaign that utilizes several marketing tactics.

### 3. Focus on fundamentals.

As difficult as it may be to believe, *ignoring the customer* is at the top of any list of most frequent marketing mistakes. Sales professionals can be so intent on getting their message out that they fail to get it across. What do your customers want to hear? Why it's in their best interest to do business with you. Most marketing efforts fail because what the customer wants to know is unclear, hidden, or—most likely—totally ignored.

### 4. Start worrying.

Worry can be productive and should never be avoided. It's essential for continued success. Stop worrying and we let our guard down. Stop worrying and the competition grabs the advantage. Stop worrying and we make mistakes. Far from draining energy, worry is energizing. It's easy to be lulled into complacency when business is good. The so-called "worry warts" are the sales people who are restless and unsure of themselves. They're also the winners.

### 5. Increase prospecting efforts.

In good times, interest in searching for new customers often wanes. We're busy taking care of orders, and we tend to believe that the flow of new business will continue unabated. But today's success gives no guarantee that it will go on forever. Having plenty of business can cause us to believe that we're doing well because we have somehow earned it. The most appropriate time to look for new customers is when we don't need them. Cultivating prospects today fuels the new-business engine in leaner times.

### 6. Differentiate, differentiate, differentiate.

Location is the watchword in real estate; separating yourself from the competition is the key in marketing. *Differentiation* is the magic word. Those who look alike are alike in customers' minds. Your tasks are: (1) find distinctions that make a difference to your customers and (2) stress these distinctions in everything you do. Schick, the number-two razor company, emphasizes a safe shave, an issue that's particularly important to teen and African American males. The appearance-conscious teens want to avoid nicks, and some African American males reportedly find shaving painful because of a condition that causes skin bumps. Gillette wins the close-shave race, but Schick goes after niche markets where safety is an issue.

### 7. Use your sales staff effectively.

Although sales professionals can display prima donna-like behavior and even a certain amount of arrogance, they are justified when they complain about much of what they're asked to do. Rather than spending time cultivating prospects, servicing existing customers, and building relationships, they are expected to make cold calls and locate new prospects. Every sales professional should be watching out for new opportunities, but spending time looking for a needle in a haystack is a waste of talent. Selling efficiency starts with good leads, and it's the job of the company to develop them. The goal is to keep the sales professionals busy doing what they do best—selling.

### 8. Offer response hooks.

A response hook is nothing more than an opportunity for the recipients of your communications—via newsletters, ads, direct mail, or the Internet—to inquire, request, or respond. Whether a request is for information, a brochure, white paper, a sample, or an appointment, offer choices because this is the moment of maximum motivation. The goal is to pull the prospects closer to you through the ways you meet their needs. Pertinent and helpful information that aids prospects can be a powerful hook.

### 9. Refuse to get sidetracked.

Staying focused isn't easy. There are powerful forces pulling and pushing in every direction except forward. Boredom causes the mind to look for new excitement. Just trying to keep up with the competition directs energy away from the goal. Ego obscures valid objectives. Getting off course, particularly when business is good, is easy, but it's also costly in the long run.

### 10. Offer something "new and improved."

Customers want to do business with sales professionals who are leaders. Although "new and improved" applies mainly to products and services, it also encompasses your marketing communications. If your letterhead, business cards, and brochures haven't changed in a number of years, you may be giving customers and prospects an impression that you are caught in a time warp. Businesses, as well as what they sell, need to have a "new and improved" look.

### 11. Tune in with technology.

There was a time when you could take a "wait-and-see" attitude toward technology. Not today. The changes are too fast and fundamental. If you're behind the curve, it's difficult—if not impossible—to catch up. The goal of technology is twofold: operating in real time, and maximizing efficiency. Today's customers won't tolerate delays and inconvenience.

### 12. Communicate constantly and consistently.

People are too busy today to remember who you are and what you do. Employees change positions frequently, and the new faces don't know you. We're so focused on what we're doing now that we don't have time to think about what's coming tomorrow or next month. If you're not available when there's a need, someone else may get the order. Be sure to stay visible to prospects and customers in a variety of ways that grab attention quickly and powerfully.

### 13. Extend your territory.

Anyone who says "We don't go farther than a half-day's drive" is doomed. The task today is to figure out ways to capture more business, and that means finding a wide market. At one time, the horse defined a market area, then the streetcar, the automobile, and the airplane. Now, the Internet has abolished all parameters. Where you are is not nearly as important as what you are to a customer.

### 14. Stay on course.

People are easily bored today. Perhaps the culprit is information overload. Whatever the cause, the effects are felt in businesses. Everything's shortterm, and even the short-term gets shorter and shorter, especially regarding our ability to develop and implement business, marketing, and sales strategies. When the results aren't instant, we move on to something new. However, successful marketing strategies are based on cumulative results, and those take time. Compared to earlier buyers, today's customers take far longer to make their buying decisions, so it's critical to be with them at the right moment, and this means staying on course.

### 15. Start thinking.

Serious thought is rare in business. Taking time to gather, review, and consider information is essential. This is why every business can profit from a contrarian—someone who offers the opposite of the popular and accepted view. Pushed aside, passed over, and ignored, these people are an endangered species. They wear the most devastating label of all: "Not a team player." The irony is that every business needs more of them. They stimulate thinking, force us to analyze our assumptions, and challenge us to look beyond our prejudices. It's better business to be known as a thinking organization.

George Will's book, *Men at Work: The Craft of Baseball,* has only four chapters (as does this book). The final chapter is called "Cal Ripken's Information." It's an amazing, audacious, and un-expected title. Here's why: "I like to learn the opposing team's hitters and our pitchers, so I can cut down on the area I have to cover. I'm not blessed with the kind of range that a lot of infielders have. So how I succeed is by THINKING," says living legend Cal Ripken. In a day when strategy is everything, so is thinking.

Rather than just rising with the tide (or falling with it), these fifteen tactics for taking control of your destiny give you the ad-vantage you need in good times and bad. No one wants outside forces to control a business, but it's easy to let the economy, com-petition, and other agents dictate your business practices. If you use the right techniques, this doesn't need to happen.

## Turn a Cold Canvass into a Hot Sale

At no time is the persuasive ability of the sales professional put to a more severe test than when an interview is conducted with a customer who has been approached as a cold canvass—via door-bell ringing or telephone calling. A cold canvass may involve searching for a means of reaching an individual whom you do not know and who, as far as you know, has expressed no interest whatsoever in you or your product.

The importance of laying the foundation for a successful sale *before* meeting prospects can't be emphasized enough. Showman-ship, friendship, publicity, and integrity—these are the stones in that foundation. Why, then, is cold canvass the real challenge of selling?

After all is said and done, the moment an individual enters a store, a sale is half made. Some of the persuasion that brings a person through the doors at a given time and for a given purpose is a result of intricate salesmanship through the advertising columns of newspapers, promotional plans, window displays, public relations, and years of struggle to build up good will in the community.

This is not to imply that there is no difference between one sales professional and another in the store, or that it makes no difference what approach is used when customers come to a display counter. They can be ignored or repelled, or they can be captivated by the seller's personality and sales talk. They may be sold something that they did not want (and will return the following week), or they may be persuaded to part with twice as much money as they had intended to spend.

These particular customers, let us emphasize, have not said "No." If they had said "No" to themselves, they would never have come to the store nor sought a particular department. (Of course, another type of salesmanship—promotion and advertising—may have turned their "No" to "Maybe" and then to "Yes.") The act of crossing the store's threshold is a way of saying "Yes" before the sale begins. And if the sale never materializes, something is wrong with the store, its merchandise, or its sales professional.

Cold canvassing starts with just the opposite attack. No customers come to the product. The product has to go out and find the customers. In fact, they aren't even customers or clients; at best, they are only prospects. Even then, we are stretching the meaning of the word, because they are prospects only insofar as everybody in the world is a prospect. In cold canvassing, the sales professional is approaching a *prospective* prospect. The sales professional goes to this individual without invitation and without encouragement.

Have you ever stopped to consider what percentage of the total American merchandise is sold to people who have expressed no previous interest? For years, the company that was far in the lead in the brush industry never placed its products in the stores. Nobody could buy even a single model of the innumerable Fuller brushes except from the sales professional who knocked on the door. The same is true of vacuum cleaners. Electrolux, for years, permitted its machine to be sold exclusively through the house-to-house technique. Refrigerators were sold in this manner when they were in competition with the iceman. Today, the home-freezing units, with and without food plans, are presented by trained people who use cold canvassing in more ways than one. If you go to a bookstore and ask for a set of *Encyclopedia Britannica,* you won't get it. This and other reference works are available only from a person who will come to your door.

The doorknockers are not sales professionals to whom clients come and say: "I want your product. How much is it and when can I get delivery?" Customers must be persuaded that they want not only something they haven't asked for, but something that they will almost invariably protest that they can't use, have no room for, and certainly cannot afford. And, to top it all, sales professionals have to show them that they have the best buy in a line—when they are not sure that they want *anything* in the line!

No wonder, then, that the bell ringers and the doorknockers have proved to be among the best potential sales professionals in this country, and have graduated from these ranks to far bigger and more important tasks. Canvassing was their proving ground, their training ground.

Cold canvassing illustrates almost everything that can be said about selling. The sale begins when the customer says "No." In fact, in cold canvassing, if the customer does *not* start in by saying, "No, I'm not interested," then something has surely gone astray. It is so much a normal part of the repartee that many sales professionals would be at a loss to continue an interview if they did not meet this expected resistance.

In the cold canvass, the first prerequisite is enthusiasm. Those who want to break down the hard wall of resistance must be bubbling over with ardor and pride in their product. They must be a living flame, aglow with warmth. They must have gusto in their voice and vehemence in their arguments. Their product reflects this passionate zeal; it takes on all the qualities of the sales professional as a matter of reflection. It becomes a wondrous and beautiful thing that is truly indispensable, and the opportunity to make the purchase cannot be bypassed without insulting one's intelligence.

Resistance? Customers are filled with resistance. They are naturally skeptical about anything that sales professionals might say. But why allow them to say so when the entire course of conversation can be under the control of the sales professionals? The more prospects are given the opportunity to voice their objections, the more they become concrete and crystallized in their own mind—particularly in the early part of an interview.

All this sounds like good theory, but how can it be put into practice? Consider this a prime rule: Never allow the conversation to lag during the cold canvass. In the breakdown of sales resistance, periods of silence are ammunition for the prospects. They will have plenty of time to reflect—after they have changed from prospects to customers. Why permit them the opportunity of unlimited hesitation now?

It would seem that the cold canvass must be direct and to the point. Everything said about indirect selling, about talking around the subject, about leading up to it subtly, about bringing clients to the point where they demand that they be sold, might seem to be inapplicable when one is face-to-face with a complete stranger. But this is not the case. The general methods are simply adapted to a specific situation.

For example, even the opening wedge after ringing the door-bell need not necessarily be a statement of the purpose of the call. "Are there any children in this home?" you might ask when selling a product designed to meet the needs of some young people. To many, it might seem that such an opening question has little or no advantage over this more direct approach: "I have here something that I would like to show you, a product that will prove very valuable to your children." Yet these two openers are actually miles apart.

Assume that there are no children in the home; the answer to the opening question is negative. Sales professionals can then inquire about friends and neighbors who have children and who therefore might be interested in a particular piece of merchandise. If the statement is used instead, the prospect may be invited to close the door after a curt reply that there are no children here and there is no interest in the product. With the question, sales professionals have offered nothing, not even an announcement that they are sales professionals. They have merely asked a question, and anyone with a civil manner would answer: "Yes, we have kids here; why?" The prospect gets no opportunity to say that he or she doesn't want the merchandise or the sales talk. With the statement, sales professionals are practically inviting the customer, who has certainly not been sold on the product, to say, "Sorry, I'm not interested," and close the door.

Let's suppose sales professionals get an affirmative answer to their question. They then proceed to ask how many children there are, and their ages; meanwhile, they are preparing their presentation. They are creating a favorable atmosphere for the sale just as surely as people who sell equipment or insurance and take great pains to have themselves and their firm known to the prospect before making the first call.

Furthermore, the sales professional is arousing the curiosity of the customer, who, in a very few moments, will want to know the purpose of the visit. This inquiry, coming from the prospect, is an invitation to tell the story and is therefore a pledge that it will be listened to.

Now let us assume that the product is rather expensive for the market being canvassed. The area is middle-class, at best, and the average family cannot afford to dispose of substantial dollars, even on a time-payment plan, without feeling a severe pinch. The mother or father is almost certain to ask the price before the presentation has been made, so astute sales professionals must know how to ignore those questions. Aquiver as they are with infatuation for their story, and eloquence for its presentations, they must continue without being sidetracked into the dangerous domain of price. They must offer little or no opportunity for interruption of their words or their train of thought. They have spread out all their brochures and pamphlets, and they talk of their product as if it were the most indispensable commodity in existence.

There is a time for the discussion of price, as well as other objections, but it should always be after the seed of the sale has been implanted on the prospect.

To lead sales professionals through every twist that an interview might take would be impossible, just as one can never outline every possible chess game, because each move can be followed by an almost endless variety of responses. But let's suppose that, in the very first moments of the presentation, when sales professionals announce what they are offering, they are told that the family already has such an item. It is generally agreed that one reference work for children (or one vacuum cleaner or one home freezing unit) is sufficient for a family, so most sales people would consider the call wasted. They would pack the few belongings that had just begun to emerge from the briefcase and, with a word of thanks, they would depart, somewhat discouraged and already figuring out how much time they had lost.

Lost? How shortsighted! A golden opportunity is presenting itself! The resident of the home interrupts to announce that the family has the particular product being sold. "You have one of these in your home? That's fine. And are you satisfied with it? Do the children feel happy with it? Do they make much use of it?" These are a few of the questions that may be asked. The answers, which will almost invariably be in the affirmative, give sales professionals a chance to urge the customer to recommend other families with children. "Surely there are other families—friends, neighbors, relatives—that would want to have this same opportunity for their children! Would you mind giving me their names so that they might have a chance to learn of this offer?"

With their fervor still at a high pitch, and consumed by their exuberance toward their own story, sales professionals can, at this point, obtain leads that will make the next calls a little less cold. Not content with obtaining names and addresses, they can impart enough of their own inspiration to get the prospect to take the initiative and call some of his or her contacts in order to make an appointment and introduce the sales professional. This is ideal, but it is by no means far-fetched.

Let's return to the interview in which the customer displays an interest, but always with the mental reservation that the product is too expensive. "No, I don't think we can afford that," he or she interrupts several times to say, and, with studied deafness, these interruptions are ignored as if they had not been at all audible. While prospects are attempting to concentrate on the price, sales professionals are seeking to discover the children's interests in specialized fields and subjects, in the hope of tying in such interest with the product being offered.

This technique can be applied widely, not just in sales for children, but, with only the slightest variations, for selling a large variety of other products for which the cold canvass must be turned into a hot sale.

House-to-house and door-to-door selling is similar in almost every respect to the method employed in selling to industrial firms. The greatest single difference is this, as I see it: In selling to an individual who has a firm, sales professionals will make contacts and friendships that will enable them to sow the seeds for a sale at one time and reap the harvest many months or even years later. Perhaps you have sold to people for the first time after having known them and visited them for many years. Perhaps during this period you had mentally written them off as prospects, believing that the possibilities of doing business with them had become remote.

In cold canvassing, one cannot wait years, or even months, for a reply. The sale must be closed almost immediately after it is opened. A frontal attack becomes necessary when one is making a visit for the first time, often against the will and judgment of the prospect. The only sure closing is the one you've accomplished. "I will think this over and let you know" is only a polite manner—whether the prospect is aware of it or not—of saying "No."

While the fervently narrated story is ringing in prospects' ears, give them the forms to sign, and obtain a deposit. While the brochures are plainly visible and the samples are opened and have been demonstrated, go for the prospects' commitment. "Think it over? Why not tell me your objections and hesitations so that we can discuss them now?"

Some people object that this procedure leads to a premature decision that may be regretted later, and therefore it will turn into a cancellation. Naturally, if the product being sold is inexpensive, no cancellation is expected. There will be an exchange of dollars-for-product, and the sale has been made. Assuming that nothing was misrepresented, it is most unlikely that the buyers will change their minds and demand the return of their money.

When larger sums are involved, customers who are persuaded to sign during the first interview may eventually cancel, but this also occurs rarely. Psychologically, a cancellation is a backward step—an admission of error. Even more than the original motion forward, this action is held back by inertia.

What happens if customers think they have been oversold and hence become dissatisfied? Is this not the worst possible advertising for a product? Not at all! Persuasive argumentation, or even overselling and high-pressure salesmanship, does not in any way imply that a product of inferior quality is being offered, or that it will fail to do what is claimed for it.

Assuming that the product is everything that the sales professional has said it is, and everything that the literature described (or more, because the literature and the samples can never be entirely adequate), the persuasion recommended does not consist of exaggeration of qualities or of misrepresentation. It consists of presenting the truth about the product with such contagious eagerness and earnestness that the prospect will buy it. It consists of answering some arguments and ignoring others, and of bringing up each issue at the proper time—the time of the sales professional's choosing, not the customer's.

Lest anyone be left with the impression that these brief remarks about cold canvassing are applicable only to house-to-house professionals selling household goods, consider this experience of a sales professional who was selling plaster for a large manufacturer of building materials. He was living in the northwest suburbs of New York City and commuting on the West Shore Railroad.

> One evening, I was on the West Shore ferry boat on my way to the Weehawken terminal, when the thought came to me that the people doing the building repair work on the Commodore Hotel might be ready to place an order for their plaster. I got off the ferry, took the next boat back, boarded a 42nd Street crosstown bus, and got off at First Avenue. I walked up to 45th Street, where I met the contractor handling the job.
>
> I came to the contractor that day without invitation, without a lead, with no knowledge that he wanted plaster at the time. But I had a long talk with him, urged him to place

the order immediately, and when he informed me that he had been planning to place it in a few weeks, I knew that my best chance would be if he gave it to me then and there. This he did, and I immediately wired it to headquarters in Chicago. It was a very large order for me, and it thrilled me so much I never forgot it.

Here were seizure of an opportunity and insistence on the immediate order, both of which are keys to a successful cold sale.

Let's give you another story—an experience of a young sales professional who was later to become one of America's more successful selling executives.

On one of my first selling trips out of town, when I was about 20 years of age, I visited a little spot on the map of Rhode Island where the company had a prospect that had been turned over to me.

It was necessary to get a local train out of Providence, and I made the youthful mistake of telephoning the proprietor for an appointment in order not to gamble on his presence at the plant on my arrival. He listened while I introduced myself over the telephone, and then in a very harsh voice said, "I don't need any of your materials," and he hung up.

I took the first train I could to his town and walked into his plant just as he was getting ready to leave for Providence in his automobile. Again I introduced myself, and he said, "Didn't I tell you over the telephone that I wasn't interested in any of your goods? Why did you come down here?" I said that this was my first trip and that I wanted to meet him, regardless of whether he bought any goods or not. He said, "Well, hop in and I'll take you back to Providence in my car."

On the way down to Providence, he became more mellow, warmed up to the conversation, asked me a good deal about my selling ambitions, and gave me the opportunity to tell him that I had come up to see him with a very special value that my company had given me to help me on my first trip and that I hoped he would at least listen to what I had to offer.

This he did, and then he made me an offer at a price slightly lower than the one that I had been authorized to quote. I told him that I did not have the authority to take the business, but that if he would allow me to take it back to the home office, I would telegraph him the next day stating whether my company could accept his bid. The order was rather sizable, and I could not get back to New York fast enough to take it up with my employer. The next day, I was able to wire the customer that the company had accepted his bid. This was the start of many years of profitable business with this company.

What does the story illustrate? First, it was a cold canvass. Second, the sales professional was imbued with eloquent enthusiasm for the product. She herself was sold on it. Third, she did not hear the first "No," nor even the second one. In fact, the sale began when the prospect said "No!"

## Four High-Performance Skills

There are no quick fixes that can guarantee increased productivity. To move from a self-imposed sales plateau to the summit of high achievement demands that you acquire the skills and behaviors of the true high achievers.

Good news: Very few people are born as high achievers, but you can practice and learn the skills that allow you to join this elite group. Increased productivity is directly and positively correlated with the successful development and the skillful utilization of four high-performance skills:

1. Increasing positive self-esteem.

2. Choosing to be voluntarily accountable to peers.

**3.** Selling from a behavioral versus a feeling agenda.

**4.** Connecting your beliefs and your behaviors.

## 1. Increasing Positive Self-Esteem

There is a direct link between a sales professional's level of positive self-esteem and income earned. Even more critical is a solid connection between a person's sense of well-being and a financially healthy sales career. Individuals who accumulate high levels of self-esteem tend to build successful practices. In contrast, persons who experience low levels of positive self-esteem tend to have volatile, unpredictable careers resulting in early plateauing and career termination.

Positive self-esteem may be the single most important factor affecting the successful selling of any product. The good news is that self-esteem can be raised! You are not condemned to see or feel in ways that limit or destroy your performance. It is not easy to increase positive self-esteem, but it is possible. Two skills can be employed to help you boost your self-esteem: (1) million-dollar feedback and (2) baby risks.

### *Million-Dollar Feedback*
Sociological and psychological literature indicates that the majority of us, throughout our entire lives, will develop only 8 to 10 percent of our natural human potential and talent. One of the reasons we do not achieve any more than this meager percentage is that we do not get enough unqualified positive feedback. Top sales associates who acquire this skill are keenly aware of some components of million-dollar feedback (so named because of a belief that the successful and consistent use of the skill will create a significant difference in economic growth over the years). Those components are:

✓ Feedback is not advice.

✓ Feedback is describing what you see, without placing any values on your perception.

✓ Feedback is most effective when it comes from a person you trust.

✓ Feedback is for the benefit of the receiver, who can use it or reject it.

✓ Feedback focuses on the positive "hidden" potential that is unknown to the receiver.

✓ Feedback is best received in a climate of trust, openness, and confidentiality.

Ninety percent of buying decisions are made at the nonverbal level. Skillful feedback allows you to tap into the powerful world of nonverbal buying. Feedback is the primary skill to access this level of selling. You cannot master the skill of feedback alone. To ignore this dynamic dimension of selling is to say, "I am blind." Without feedback, you are not only blind, you are guaranteeing yourself high levels of mediocrity. You can discover only a fraction of your potential without the perception, support, insight, and love of important people in your life. You need the gift of feedback; it is truly an explosive and powerful tool of highly successful sales professionals.

### *Baby Risks*

We live in a basically no-risk culture. The general assumption of the sales profession is that when you make sales your career, you are a real risk taker. Many sales professionals are trapped in production levels significantly below their desires and their experience capabilities because they fear risk—and they fear risk because they have no risking skills, they don't understand risk, and they lack a support climate that challenges them to live at the growth edge of their capability.

Rabbi Harold Kushner helps us grasp the results of a no-risk lifestyle: "We become emotionally anesthetized. We learn to live our whole life within a narrow emotional range, accepting the fact [that] there will be few high spots in exchange for the guarantee there will be no low moments, no pain or sadness, just a perpetual feeling of monotony, one gray day after another. Choosing a no-risk lifestyle is in itself a tragic risk." To understand the awesome tragedy of passive, no-risk living is the first step in taking "baby risks."

In a speech delivered at an MDRT annual meeting, psychologist Charles Garfield provides a valuable risk skill that he refers to as the "catastrophic consequence report." The skill focuses on some tough questions that can be used to sort through a challenge or decision you may face. Among these questions are: "What is the worst possible scenario with the risk I am considering?" "Am I willing to live with all the potential outcomes?" "Am I willing to accept responsibility for the results?" Choosing to practice this skill regularly, with issues that are important but not life-altering, is the process that high achievers use to gain confidence as risk takers.

You can become a successful risk taker by adding a risk list to your annual goals. This list can include physical, professional, or interpersonal risks.

As an example of a physical risk, let's say you want to lower your golf handicap. Here's what you might do from a behavioral standpoint:

1. Take five lessons from a PGA professional in the next three months.

**2.** Hit balls at the driving range weekly, for one hour.

**3.** Play in two tournaments.

Here's an example of a professional risk. Let's say you want to upgrade your client base. Here's what you might do from a behavioral standpoint. Ask for appointments with ten individuals who earn in excess of $100,000 annually. Positive self-esteem can be raised by developing and using the skills of million-dollar feedback and baby risks.

## 2. Choosing to Be Voluntarily Accountable to Peers

The majority of sales professionals place independence near the top of the list when they talk about the benefits and perks in their profession. For many, independence has become a liability. If you are really honest with yourself, admit that you are not extremely disciplined. The more willing you are to share your goals with others and ask them to support you and hold you accountable, the more likely you are to achieve and even surpass your standards.

There isn't one best way to make yourself accountable, but there is a positive connection between higher levels of production and increased voluntary accountability to peers. The following factors, when implemented, can enhance accountability:

**1.** Accept the reality that human beings are not very disciplined.

**2.** Reflect on the majority of your past successes (academic, athletic, arts, job, community, etc.). Were they not accomplished in the context of a team?

**3.** Accept the reality that peer groups and study groups are generally not designed for high accountability.

4. If your goals and sales behaviors are not quantified in written form and shared with important people, most likely you will not achieve them.

5. Valuable people bring out your best efforts.

6. By stating your goals and dreams to important people, you can achieve each of them.

7. A sales career can often result in isolation. It a tough and lonely business, even on good days. You need support and accountability. Performers who practice accountability develop the skill of quick course correction. It is not fatal to get off course; that's to be expected. It is fatal to a sales career to *not know* that you are off course, or to be off course and not know how to self-correct.

8. To achieve your maximum potential in a sales career, you need to trade some of the independence myth for accountability reality.

9. For many people, the need to belong is an especially strong motivator. Belonging and accountability may be the two resources needed to move to the next level of production. Without voluntary accountability, you have plateaued.

## 3. Selling from a Behavioral versus a Feeling Agenda

Sales professionals tend to build their careers on feelings instead of behaviors. A sales career founded on feelings operates on the assumption that strong positive feelings are required to make calls and to deal with the normal rejection that is predictable in the business. An alternative is to build the foundation of one's career on a fixed set of daily, weekly, and monthly behaviors.

Some sales professionals falsely buy into the notion that a strong positive mental attitude will automatically produce a strong bias for positive sales action and behavior. This is a myth and a critical mistake to buy into. It works exactly the opposite. Selecting and practicing effective sales behavior over a consistent period of time will generate positive feelings about the behavior.

Good, warm, positive feelings will not consistently produce adequate sales action. Consistent sales behavior, regardless of the feelings associated with the behavior, will consistently produce good, warm, positive feelings.

Positive feelings will not always generate positive behavior, yet positive behavior will always generate positive feelings. Ask serious runners to talk about their feelings and behaviors relating to running. "Do you feel like getting up at 6 A.M., five days a week, to run?" Most will answer, "No, not all of the time." Then ask, "Do you run whether you feel like it or not?" They will most likely respond, "Yes." Follow that with, "After you run, how do you feel?" Overwhelmingly, you will hear, "Engaged, relaxed, good!"

The feeling/behavioral challenge is a major battleground for most sales professionals. Your success in moving more closely to a behavioral system will provide a foundation for increased production.

A primary reason you get caught in the "feeling trap" instead of operating out of a more predictable behavioral model is that you are confused about what you have been taught about human motivation. Most industries confuse motivation with stimulation. Motivation is often defined as a feeling. In reality, motivation is an internal process; it is one's ability to validate oneself.

Motivation is synonymous with self-love. To motivate oneself is to care for, believe in, and have respect for one's own value. Motivation is not dependent on how one feels, it is dependent on how one acts toward oneself. *You* are the only person on the planet Earth who can motivate you!

Stimulation is more of an external experience. Food, music, applause, sports, beautiful people—all of these can be stimulants, but not motivators. High achievers pay the price to carefully distinguish between internal motivation and external stimulation. Careers built on stimulation will experience the proverbial roller coaster syndrome. Stimulation careers are built on feeling foundations. Motivated careers are built on behavior/action foundations. The choice of a career foundation is of supreme importance. Perhaps your career needs a more stable foundation. It is tough to rebuild a foundation, but it is tougher and more costly to continue to rely on one based on feelings.

Check your emotional bank balance. Can you afford to feel the way you feel? Performers act their way through life. Nonperformers feel their way through life.

## 4. Connecting Your Beliefs and Your Behaviors

High performers possess a crystallized belief system about who they are and what they do. Average performers reflect murky beliefs and inconsistent behaviors. As a sales professional, you should challenge your belief system, especially what you believe about the products you sell. Do a reliable check of your belief system; look honestly at how you spend the majority of your time. A surgeon who spends three hours a week in surgery would not be your number-one choice if you were to face open-heart surgery.

Higher performance is generated when there is close interaction between one's belief and one's behavior. High achievers in any profession waste very little energy because of a discrepancy between beliefs and behavior. Two examples of real people will illustrate this connection. The first person devoted most of his life to becoming the best cowboy he could become. His friends called him Rope, and so did his children. Shortly before he died, he was asked about how his beliefs related to his life's work as a cowboy. His immediate response: "It's the only thing I ever wanted to do. I loved it." Rope's beliefs were his actions, and his actions mirrored his beliefs.

The second person is the boxing trainer, Angelo Dundee. During an interview, a reporter was probing Dundee about why he never became a boxing promoter or a trainer who owned the contracts of the athletes. Dundee's response, "I did not want to be a promoter or an owner; I wanted to be the best corner man in the world, between those three-minute rounds. I wanted to be the best in the world for that one minute." His record says that he probably was the best. He acted on his beliefs, and his beliefs allowed him to stay focused on his actions. Diffusion and distraction are unknown issues to the Ropes and the Dundees of the world.

We become what we believe if we act on our beliefs.

## Audio Techniques for Self-Imposed Goal Setting

Have you ever attended a workshop or presentation and heard a great speaker who really motivated you? While you were listening, did you become energized and enthused? Was it clear to you just how you could become the person you have always dreamed of becoming?

Were you truly motivated, only to find that, three or four days later, the feeling began to wane, and one week later it was gone completely?

This common experience illustrates what any sales professional has already discovered. Motivation simply doesn't last very long. It is very much like exercise. If you stop doing it regularly, the benefits quickly evaporate.

Studies of some of the largest U.S. financial services companies have led researchers to notice that their top sales professionals share several personal characteristics. One of the most pronounced of these traits is a desire for continual self-motivation.

On a regular basis, these high-ranked sales professionals engage in some activity that keeps their mind focused on the goals they are attempting to achieve. Some of them repetitiously write their objectives down on paper, to plant them in their subconscious mind. By having their goals in writing, they are able to focus on them visually as well as kinesthetically. In a relatively short period of time, that repetition will create a long-lasting memory, so their focus on the targets and their production efforts toward the goals will increase.

As simple and as outstanding as this technique is, most people will not take the time and effort to do it long enough to have any positive effect. The efficacy of "spaced repetition" is well known, but actually writing something down over and over is long and laborious.

In a popular variation of this technique, you write down your goals once; develop a game plan by deciding what you need to do to actually achieve these objectives, script it all out, and then make copies. Post the copies in places where you are likely to see them frequently, and reread them or recite them when you see them. This spaced-repetition approach will drive the information into your mind. (Some people will not do it because they don't want the responsibility of others' knowing what they have committed to doing.) Repetitiously visualizing your goals is another way of imbedding them in your subconscious mind.

## An Alternative Method

Another equally effective approach is rarely used by sales professionals, even though it solves many of the problems inherent with the other spaced-repetition techniques. Consider this: How many hours a week do you spend driving around in your car? Most cars these days come with a tape player already installed. How difficult would it be for you to script out your business objectives, turn them into written affirmations, and then verbally dub them onto a cassette tape? If you want to make the feedback even more effective, have soft, rhythmic music playing in the background while you read your goal-scripts onto tape. The music will create a physical state of relaxation and help you get your mind in focus.

What would be the advantages of putting your goals on tape? The first obvious advantage is that you only have to do it once, and then you can listen to them endlessly. Second, this is a passive approach to internalizing goals. Once the tape is made, you don't have to listen to it—that is, you don't have to stop driving, pull your car off the road, and carefully listen to what is on your tape in order to get the benefits of it. Instead, when you are driving to an appointment, you can have the tape playing in the background without even paying attention to it, and you will still pick up what is on the tape.

The best examples of this "passive learning" are TV commercials. See if you can fill in the blanks: "Winston tastes good, like _____," or "Please don't squeeze _____," and "Fly the friendly skies of _____." Did you try to learn these commercials? Did you want to learn them, and will you ever be able to forget them? These messages became deeply imbedded in your subconscious mind simply because they were consistently droning in the background. Presumably, you did not sit down one day and tell yourself, "I am going to learn the Charmin bathroom tissue commercial today," but there it is, recognizable and repeatable.

Advertisers pay fortunes to drive commercial messages into your subconscious. They know that the more focused you are on *anything,* the more likely you are to do something about it. If you are walking down the aisle at a grocery store and you notice a product, the commercial message for that product will come to mind. If the message can focus you for as little as one second, the likelihood of your purchasing the product or service goes up dramatically.

To really drive the point home, here are two more examples of how getting focused on something changes the way you see the world.

Have you ever purchased a new car and then suddenly noticed that the same year and model car is in a hundred driveways? The act of purchasing the vehicle drove that information into your subconscious, and you suddenly noticed how many other people were driving the same kind of car.

How well you focus your subconscious influences whether you will achieve your business goals this year. Put simply, the more focused you are on setting appointments, the more likely that you will notice the telephone on your desk when you sit down. Many "unfocused" sales professionals notice the newspaper or incoming mail, and read it for a few minutes. The more focused you are on asking for referrals, the more likely you will "see" the client as a source of good, quality leads.

One of the biggest advantages of goal setting with tapes is how remarkably versatile you can make the content. One month, you could choose to work on a production goal; the following month, you can work on qualifying for a company contest. Many sales professionals are already habitual listeners of other people's motivational messages. Why not make your own? The tapes can be listened to while driving, working out, taking a walk, fishing, or doing paperwork. What could be simpler?

Committing your goals to tape is an easy four-phase process:

1. Write down your goals (daily, midrange, and long-term).

2. Develop a reasonable strategy for achieving them.

3. Turn the goals into a set of written, positive affirmations.

4. Transfer the goal script onto a tape.

Getting your goals on tape affords a simple, hands-on approach that really works well with your busy schedule. Motivation doesn't come easily, but if you can't motivate *yourself,* how can anyone else motivate you?

## Mind-Shift Marketing

In the past month, have you said, "Never mind, I'll do it myself!"? Do you question where you should put your time? Should it be spent in problem solving? Personnel? Training? Client service? Continuing education? Selling? After lots of hard work, do you find that you're doing well, but you don't know how to take your business to the next level?

If you are connecting with any of these questions or situations, it's a sign that you are too busy working *in* your business—rather than working *on* your business. Let's examine some of the most productive business-building marketing strategies used throughout the world. They have already resulted in a 100 percent increase in profitability within a twelve-month period, in a multitude of situations.

### The Paradox of Progress

To successfully build your business beyond your highest expectations, you must understand something called the Paradox of Progress. If you open the door to history and look back about one hundred years, you'll see the genesis of The Age of Industrialism. Commensurate with that age is a concept called the Concentration of Power. In that era, the population became increasingly focused on *big*—big business, big factories, big government, big houses, big cars. This caused the masses of American employees to gradually adjust to and accept job descriptions, routines, assignments, and authority as a part of this positioning toward power. In exchange for their loyalty, many Americans received job security and could depend on the federal government to provide a meaningful retirement benefit.

To maximize the usefulness of this information today, you must be equally cognizant of the creative destruction that has affected many employees during the past hundred years. Some crafts, such as watchmaking and blacksmithing, have all but disappeared. Telephone operators and railroad employees are on the brink of elimination.

What does this have to do with being a sales professional today? Plenty! The projections are that, within two decades, over 80 percent of the jobs available in the United States will be cerebral, and only 20 percent will be manual—the exact opposite of the ratio in 1900. You are now part of the Age of the Knowledge Worker, and you must create new marketing techniques to work successfully in this era. You must also be aware that those to whom you market have lost the sense of security their parents knew; they are awash with feelings of fear and uncertainty. Therefore, your message to them must be one that stirs feelings of confidence and reassures them about an exciting future.

In spite of the destruction of certain occupations, a safety net of eight million new jobs has been created since 1900. Professions such as medical technologists, computer programmers and technicians, airline pilots, and mechanics didn't even exist in 1900! Today, millions of Americans are employed in these new professions.

Accompanying this shift from brawn to brain is the end of *big*. We are in a transition toward smaller business, smaller factories, and smaller government. The Age of Industrialism is extinct; the Age of the Individual reigns. Marketing techniques of the past need to be buried alongside the rusting components of yesterday. You can no longer count on your corporate headquarters to effectively market for you. You must develop an entirely new set of survival strategies for the new century.

## Used-To's and How-To's

The list of "used-to's" needs to be replaced with the updated "how-to's." For example, you used to be taught to market your company. You used to believe that "bigger was better." Current marketing strategies call for you to market yourself and your individual practices if you want to bond with those who are independently building their futures and their fortunes.

Sales professionals used to have exclusive access to certain information. Back then, they could market a product. Today, because information is more readily available to all, you must do market partnering. You may serve as the "coach" for the products and services you sell, but everyone has access to the game book. You used to market mostly to the left brain—the logical side—of prospects when you considered charts and calculations with them. The new century's focus must be more holistic; you must combine the head and the heart, business and baby, personal and philanthropic, if you expect to even be in the business ten years from today.

Perhaps, at one time, you used to tell your clients you could do it all. Not anymore! You must become a specialist and develop and market strategic alliances with other experts in this increasingly complex world.

## Where to Market

Before you attempt to develop any marketing effort, you must clearly define whom you want as your clients. You can define them by industry, profession or occupation, age, income, or net worth, but you must define them or you cannot serve as their specialist. How will you know whom you want as clients? By answering questions like these:

- ✓ What do I most enjoy doing?
- ✓ How can my business be integrated with my personal philosophies?

✓ Are my personal values congruent with my business practices?

✓ Do I have a mission statement for myself and my family?

✓ What is important to me?

✓ Do I have a mission statement for my business?

✓ What do I stand for?

✓ What is my philosophy in dealing with staff, colleagues, clients, suppliers, and the corporate office?

What do all these answers have to do with marketing your business? Everything! Today's clients and employees are interested in building long-term relationships. Consequently, they want to work with people who are most like them because the relationships will develop more easily. Most sales professionals are so stretched for time that they prefer relationships that "immediately feel right" rather than those that take time, energy, and effort to develop.

Take the time to answer all the questions in this section. You'll be taking the important first steps toward defining your ideal customer, associate, and employee. And don't limit yourself to the traditional definition of a customer. Your ideal customer may not be an individual.

✓ Who are my competitors?

✓ What do they do that I admire?

✓ What do they do that I dislike?

✓ What do I perceive as their advantages compared to my practice?

✓ What are my advantages compared to their practice?

You'll also want to assess your present practice:

✓ How many customers do I have?

✓ How many of them are active buyers?

Compose a profile of your average customer: net worth, average purchase (dollar amount), average commission, geographic location, profession. Then answer these questions:

✓ How does this profile compare to my concept of an ideal customer?

✓ How many customers should I have?

✓ What am I presently doing that I should delegate to others?

✓ What are my three most important money-making activities?

✓ Do I have adequate technology, people, and systems on hand to sustain new growth?

✓ What needs to change if I am to go from where I am now to where I want to be?

Prospects today want long-term relationships. That requires two-way communication. Give some thought to your message to your customers:

✓ How frequently do I contact my customers? What media or settings do I use? How frequently do they buy from me?

✓ What is my referral system like?

✓ How does it work?

✓ Is it organized?

✓ What percentage of my business comes from referrals?

## Establishing Your Market

If you have primarily been a loner, you must start to form strategic alliances with others immediately. Include people within your industry as well as professionals in related fields. To do this successfully, each of you must represent an area of special service to the customer. Become an expert on something. What feature of your business do you most enjoy? Pursue it and master it! Then market yourself to others. Let them know you're available to help them when they have need for your expertise.

How do you accomplish self-marketing? Write an article on your area of special expertise for a professional publication, the local business newspaper, the daily paper, or a paper in a nearby city. Read some technical articles published for an industry that is related to your own. In a letter to the editor of a relevant publication, express and substantiate your opinion on an article or topic, especially if it is different from one that you have just read or heard. A well-stated letter is an excellent self-marketing medium.

You don't write well? Then speak! Be a guest on local radio or cable television talk shows. The sponsors of these programs are always looking for an interesting topic—and person—to air with listeners or viewers. Tell your story as frequently as possible. Speak at local, regional, or national meetings and conferences. Have your own web site—or your own radio or television show! Share it with members of your team. Get noticed! Be a consultant or a write-in question answerer to others! Ask for referrals every chance you get!

Identify people whom you would like to have on your networking team. Take them to lunch or breakfast. Explain your idea and ask whether they are interested. If they are, work together on how to develop your joint ideas so that they result in a win–win situation for all involved. If you cannot demonstrate some benefit for everyone, revise the idea or find new partners.

When the power shifts from the corporate office to your office, seize it! Use this exciting opportunity to propel your practice to new possibilities. Align yourself with clients who are most like you. Be a perpetual student. If you rest on past results, you will be replaced.

Turn excuses into excellence . . . obstacles into opportunity . . . procrastination into power . . . mediocrity into magnificence—all through mind-shift marketing!

# CONCLUSION

Salesmanship has been called the art of persuasion, and it has been responsible for every advance in the history of the world. Every great economic, social, political, and religious movement or change resulted from the ability of humans to sell their ideas to others. And any selling endeavor always requires enthusiasm toward the ideas being sold.

Enthusiasm is absolutely necessary for success as a sales professional. The power of enthusiasm is miraculous. Without it, any sales efforts and abilities are limited. To generate enthusiasm for the products and services you sell, you must feel enthusiastic. The effect starts and ends with you.

Sales professionals' success is linked to the sum of what they say and do in the sales process. Words and actions that are seemingly very small and unimportant may make the difference in your success. Conviction is the keystone in the arch that sales professionals pass through on their way to success. Sales professionals who have conviction have the courage to embrace the law of averages. They know that their sales efforts will be rewarded with more wins than losses.

A career in sales is a noble calling; without salespeople, there would be no progress. Yet hundreds of thousands of sales professionals fail to cash in on their potential ability because they lack a winning attitude and they don't contribute the effort needed to excel in their profession.

The sales professionals of The Million Dollar Round Table are proud of themselves, the career they have chosen, and the services they give customers. These high achievers, motivated by intense pride, have never wanted to see their names listed among the losers. By borrowing the spirit and the wisdom of MDRT members, you can develop a winning attitude and high sales success.

Calvin Coolidge once said, "Nothing in the world can take the place of persistence. Talent will not do it; nothing is more common than unsuccessful men and woman with talent. Genius will not; unrewarded genius is almost a proverb. Education will not; the world is full of educated derelicts. Persistence and determination alone are omnipotent."

Let that be your creed as a sales professional. Persist, and succeed well and proudly.

# A FINAL NOTE

The books in this series are based on the experience of some of the top salespeople in the world. The secrets and techniques they provide will help you to prospect, close, and sell more effectively and efficiently, and improving these skills will improve your sales ratio and thus your career. You would not have purchased this book if you were not motivated by success, but does a greater volume of sales make you successful? All of the salespeople who contributed to this book would say that sales volume leads to success, but does not define it. In fact, all of the most successful salespeople in The Million Dollar Round Table are firm adherents to the association's Whole Person Philosophy, which maintains that to meet one's highest professional potential, one must strive to meet the highest potential in all other parts of life.

A whole person is committed to a life of significance, happiness and fulfillment and understands that leading such a life requires a continual process of growth. Success in any area of life, be it familial, health, educational, career, service, financial, or spiritual, is dependent upon success in and balance with the other areas since all areas of life are intertwined.

Sales is a career that demands extraordinary dedication. The hours are arduous, the reactions of prospects can be hostile or humiliating, and the financial rewards are variable. After a long day cold calling or meeting with uncooperative prospects, it can be difficult to spend time and energy on your family, on caring for your body, or on the pursuit of further education. It is not always easy to comprehend that good health, good family relationships, and a commitment to education will enhance your sales career, but the experience of thousands of MDRT members has proved this true. When you are confident, when you are healthy, when you live by a secure code of values, and when you are able to adapt to change, you will inspire the respect and trust of your prospects, and sales will follow.

From the very beginning, a successful salesperson must demonstrate responsibility. The high producing salesperson practices responsibility to prospects, in providing them with the best product to meet their needs and their budget. In addition, a successful salesperson must be responsible to herself, in putting forth the time and effort to do the prospecting that must be done to get appointments and to be successful. An expert salesperson is also responsible to his industry, educating himself and using good moral judgment to improve the public's preconceptions about salespeople, and responsible to his community, giving time, energy, and money back to the area that provides his clients and therefore his living.

For some, the responsibilities of sales are overwhelming to the point they are ignored, which is why many sales careers are so brief. For others, the responsibility of gathering and maintaining a client base can be so wearing that other areas of responsibility become subordinate. Persistence in sales can be as dangerous as giving up if the salesperson is focused on aspects of the career that won't lead to success. Often, the highest producers spend less time at work than those who are struggling even to obtain interviews. It is difficult to know when to draw the line between a persistent person and a workaholic, and, as one MDRT member points out, frequently the training for a sales career convinces new salespeople that workaholic is synonymous with success. As he says:

The [sales] business is a unique and curious business. We are attracted to this great business because of the opportunities and the unlimited possibilities. And truly, they are unlimited. I do not know of any other occupation where the average person, equipped with desire, motivation, and discipline, can achieve an elite standard of living and still be helping others. The successes of this business are paradoxical. The personal sacrifices and undaunted discipline needed to make it in this great business are also the traits that so often turn one into a workaholic.

In the [sales] business, we, our careers, our measures as human beings in the business world, are measured by the amount of money we are able to make. In fact, in this business, our ranking as individuals is based on the amount of production we do month in and month out—and on into years. Early in my career, I had been brainwashed in the same way, and consequently money and money-oriented goals became the number one priority in my life. Now I know, in order to become a truly happy and successful individual, and salesperson, one must write down one's goals, love and serve people, and work.

Isolating oneself as a workaholic will not increase sales in the long term. Instead, concentrating on changing one's perceptions about oneself, and developing and growing in all areas of life will permanently increase your ability to gain sales. For too long the sales profession has defined success in terms of monetary goals. The Whole Person Philosophy is designed to help you meet those goals while focusing on how to develop a successful life, not just a successful production year.

# Career

A successful career is based upon four major components: discipline, vision, goals, and ethics. To become a great salesperson, one must concentrate on all four. To do this, as one MDRT producer insists, you must make a committed decision to be abnormal. Most people spend the majority of their lives striving to be normal—to fit comfortably within their community, their office, their group of friends. Why the sudden need to become different, to become other than what your peers are, to become abnormal? Because the normal people, the majority, are the status quo, who are mired in routine. To be a success, you need to be able to think outside the box, to question the routines and procedures that have always been followed "because they work," and alter them so they work even better. Unless you make a commitment to excel in your life and your business, you will be among the 80 percent who are normal, and normal is, at best, average, and, at worst, mediocre. To be a success you must be able to leave behind the comfort of rut and routine, and join the abnormal—the 20 percent minority of the population that is exploring and experimenting to create progress.

To leave the majority behind requires a tremendous amount of discipline. First, it requires the discipline to do what is difficult rather than what comes naturally: to analyze your actions and determine what works, rather than following the generally accepted procedure. Second, it requires the discipline to push outside your comfort zone in order to reach new levels of success when you are already successful. Third, it requires the discipline to realize no job is too small to be done to the best of your ability. In short, discipline is the difference between success and mediocrity. As a top producer in MDRT relates, "Successful people discipline themselves to do the things the less successful don't like to do." He continues:

> Successful people understand it isn't the big jobs which bring success. It's the little things we have to do every day. What will surprise you here is there are no extraordinary people, but some have disciplined themselves to achieve extraordinary

goals. Discipline not to go home on a Friday until the diary is full for the following week. Discipline to break down the goals into daily tasks. What do I have to do now, today, which if I repeat it day after day, will bring my goals to reality? It's what we do each day that determines our failure or success. Success is something we have to practice on a daily basis.

The discipline to become successful has to be rewarded by something, or it would be simpler to continue doing things as you have always done them. All discipline results from a vision. Those salespeople who have the discipline to make success happen a little at a time derive that discipline from seeing themselves as successful. Most people want to improve their lives and careers, in other words, most people want to be successful. In spite of this, most people are unable to discipline themselves to think and act differently, because they are unable to envision themselves as successful. A respected member of MDRT explains the importance of vision this way:

People of greatness don't get there by accident. The person who gets to the top of the mountain didn't fall there! They become masterful by making choices and decisions of exactly what it is they want to achieve. When you realize that the world we live in is entirely made up, then you are free to create the world you want. All of us know that goals sculpt and shape our lives. We know that, we've heard about their importance enough times haven't we? However, goals alone are not enough to turn your life into a masterpiece.

Many people make the mistake of just setting goals without having something greater to live for, without a deep felt purpose at the core of your very being. As George Bernard Shaw wrote, "A purpose recognized by yourself is a mighty one." We need to go beyond goal setting, because goal setting on its own has limitations.

Everything large is built up from small pieces; giant leaps are the accumulation of many smaller leaps. Realization of your vision doesn't come usually in one move, but one step at a time. The whole is the sum total of its parts. What's important is that each smaller step is a part of the big picture, otherwise you can still be a goal achiever, and not be a success.

Think of your vision as a jigsaw puzzle. It can't be done in one move, or by rushing and jamming pieces into place. The only way is by visualizing the finished image and then working piece by piece, day by day. Then what happens is as you begin to solve it the quicker and easier you complete it. You build momentum. If you build a little on a little and do this often, soon it becomes big. Without a vision the goals will not take the shape of the whole, will they?

Your daily actions and activities should come not only from your goals, but from your vision. This will give your daily activities more meaning and purpose.

Your vision of yourself provides you the motivation to complete the daily tasks that are inherent in being a successful salesperson. Goals are the way you can measure progress in reaching your vision, and the way you can focus your discipline to directly lead from where you are to where you envision yourself. As one motivational expert at an MDRT meeting said, "goals manipulate process." Achievement of your vision is dependent upon practical application of the discipline your vision has instilled in you, and goals allow you to apply that discipline.

A goal is a piece of the jigsaw puzzle that composes your vision. With each goal you meet, you are getting closer to the success you envision yourself to be, and each goal you meet makes subsequent goals easier because of the confidence attaining goals lends you. For a goal to assist you in becoming your vision, it must be realistic. It is best to start with smaller goals, such as "I will call twenty new prospects every day next week," and build up to goals like "I will be my business' highest producer this year," or the system will backfire. By setting unrealistic goals you are procrastinating on reaching your vision, since each goal that you fail to meet will make you less likely to move forward. This is not to say your goals should be things you know you can do. As one well-known motivation researcher states, goals are most effective if they have a 50 percent chance of failure:

> What research has discovered, and what could be pure gold for anyone who understood how to apply it, is that your goals will continue to strengthen your motivation up to the fifty percent probability of success. In other words, your goals are most motivating, they tap into your most powerful inner resources, when you have a 50/50 chance at reaching them, when your probability of success is fifty percent. And no motivation is aroused when the goal is perceived as being either virtually certain, or virtually impossible to attain. This provides the answer for so many sales professionals who seem to lose their achievement drive. They have failed to use goals to fuel their internal fire, to motivate themselves properly.

Goals are motivation to maintain the discipline that is used to fuel the conversion of your vision into a reality. Every time you reach a goal you are propelled to achieve more, because you have the confidence of achievement and because you have a new habit for success. According to recent research, it takes 21 days to establish a new habit. When you raise the bar to reach a goal, and are doing something every day to ensure your success, after 21 days it becomes second nature—a part of your established routine. So, even after your goal has been met, you will be in the habit of doing something that has contributed to your success. Many people focus on the end, the meeting of a goal, as the main benefit, but the adoption of habits that allow you to reach the goal are every bit as important. As many MDRT members have pointed out, success is a process, not an event. The habits you develop in pursuit of a goal will make you more successful, as will the attitude you develop from the implementation of those habits. A top member and motivational expert said:

Ongoing action supports a goal. And whenever we are in action toward a goal, we feel better about ourselves, our energy is higher, our confidence and self-esteem are growing in strength. When we coast, when our achievement drive is low, our self-esteem goes down, we retreat into our comfort zones, and lose much of our enthusiasm for life. Our attitude goes sour.

Goals are important because they improve your habits and they alter your attitude. When we are efficient and we are full of energy we are more capable of success, and the more successful we are in reaching our goals, the easier it becomes for us to set more.

While determining visions, setting goals, and using discipline to reach them, one must be certain that the vision of success is based on solid ethical principles. Becoming a success takes a great deal of work and energy, and any path to success that does not include hard work and effort is bound to be faulty. As one member of MDRT says, doing the right thing goes hand in hand with doing well. There are ways to become successful with no great investment of time and energy, but the success you will attain using these methods will be transparent and transitory. The only way to be successful is to inspire your prospects to believe in you, and this will only happen if they can see you creating successful habits and meeting goals. Instant success is possible through only the most unethical methods, that initially hurt others, but eventually will hurt the people who practice them.

Sales is a profession that is frequently accused of questionable ethics. We have all seen films or heard jokes that feature unscrupulous used car dealers, or salespeople who are thinly disguised con men. These negative stereotypes make it all the more important that your sales dealings be straightforward and honest ones. To find and keep customers you need to take personal responsibility for who you are and what you do. When your prospects see that you are someone focused on success and working hard to get there, they will feel comfortable giving you their business. When they see how your goal-oriented habits and discipline are put to work in their best interests, they will become clients, giving you more business, referring you to their friends, and contributing to your success.

This can be a slow process, and at times it will be tempting to place immediate success over honesty, integrity, and fairness. If you are to be successful in sales, you will be patient, and put in the hours and work rather than pursue personal gain through shady business dealings. A past president of MDRT told this story to emphasize how important ethics are to success:

> I think that sometimes nice guys may appear to finish last, but that's because they're running in a different race. For example, Australian golfer, Greg Norman, is one of the biggest draws on the pro tour. He was among the leaders of the 1996 Greater Hartford open, when he disqualified himself by reporting to tournament officials that he had inadvertently played with an improper ball for the first two rounds. That's ethics. There is no pillow as soft—or as comforting—as a clear conscience.

Questionable ethics may allow you to win sales in the short term, but long-term success is conditional upon loyal clients, who will only come to you when, like Norman, you admit your wrongs and prove your commitment to ethical business dealings.

To have a successful sales career you must be able to envision yourself as a success. Then, you must break your vision into smaller goals, and develop the habits and the discipline to meet them. You must live by a code of ethics that insists upon honesty, fairness, compassion, and hard work, and the sales will follow.

## Education

Education is closely related to the area of sales success. Your vision of sales success can be broken down into goals, like completing professional training or designation programs, that will increase customer confidence and therefore sales, but education is an area of life distinct from either career or play.

As the inspiration for the Whole Person Philosophy, Dr. Mortimer J. Adler, explains, education is part of an important life category known as leisure. Leisure activities are activities that provide no extrinsic gain or compensation, but rather intrinsic rewards. These activities may be extremely grueling, but are worth doing despite the difficulty of the tasks. As we must have work in order to live, we must have leisure in order to live well. Dr. Adler explains:

> Leisure activities either produce a growth in the human person, a development of the self, or they produce advances in civilization, developments in the arts and sciences. Any form of learning, any form of creative work, any form of political or socially useful activity, is a leisure activity. Anything which contributes to the advancement of society is a leisure activity. It follows, then, that leisure activities are those which are morally obligatory.

As a sales professional you serve the public as a trusted advisor, and are responsible for being up to date with current knowledge and developments in your field in order to serve your clients in the best way possible.

Pursuit of education makes you more confident with prospects, and this, in turn, increases sales. Confidence is rarely achieved through public adulation. Instead, confidence usually comes from competence, which in turn comes from knowledge. When you increase your knowledge and confidence, you become more aware of your values, behave in a more creative manner, better communicate things you believe in to others, and are able to translate ideas into action through consistent hard work. Hard work without a sense of direction leads to frustration, but education can focus your work, increase your confidence, and help you analyze and improve your professional skills. As one MDRT member asserts, our success in becoming a professional human being depends very much on the efforts we make to understand and continue our own professional self-growth and development.

We no longer have the luxury of dying in the same world into which we were born. We are undergoing constant change. A development committee at Sony determined that at the current rate of technological change a new product becomes obsolete every 18 days. To be successful in an environment like this, you need to be able to think of a way to replace that product and get it out before the eighteenth day, so that you aren't surpassed by another company. Many people carry palm pilots. These computers, small enough to fit into a shirt pocket, contain more computer technology than was available in the whole world in 1985. The world we live in demands constant education to meet the demands of its constant change. A highly respected MDRT member sums this up well when he says:

> We need to continually educate and reeducate ourselves so that our knowledge and skills are cutting edge. As business guru Alvin Toffler says, "The illiterates of the future are not those who cannot read and write, but those who cannot learn, unlearn, and relearn."

Charles Darwin says the success of a species has little to do with its size or its strength, but everything to do with its ability to adapt to changing circumstances. The same can be said of the success of a salesperson. As one motivational expert says, "In a post-industrial economy, people aren't a factor of production, people are the competitive edge. If you're not educated, it's not that you will be unimportant to the society. If you are not educated, you will be irrelevant to the society. If you are not educated, you are not working." He goes on to say:

> In a post-industrial society, schools, corporate training programs, and seminars are the farms of the future. People are the new products. You are the new crops. We taught you to believe that education was the pursuit of knowledge. All you wanted was to make an "A" on a test, to graduate on time, or get credit for going to some seminar. But education is not about the pursuit of knowledge, it's about the pursuit of significance. It's about making a difference with your life. It's about adding value to your work and those around you. It is about giving all you can give and maximizing your talents. Knowledge is something you get along the way.

Education and knowledge are important because they change your dealings with other people, especially prospects, for the better, but they are essential because they force you to deal with yourself differently. Sales careers have a tendency to force people to see their success and significance purely in terms of monetary goals, which can become difficult to meet in this era of constant change. It is a comfort to pursue higher education in situations like this, because it relieves you of the pressure inherent in equating money with success. Education does not have to be formal in order to assist you in expanding your vision of success; in fact, one MDRT member feels the education he accomplishes on his own is as helpful as enrollment in any taught program. He advises:

> I memorize one message every month. Memorizing positive statements, poems and things, really helps round out, not only one's mind, but the way one views the world, and I need to start doing more of it. What we memorize is what we become, in part, a product of.

Education forces you to expand your thinking about success and about the world and your place in it. As long as you are learning, you are growing, and growth gives you the confidence and competence you need to be successful in a world of continual change. As a long-term MDRT member says:

> Growth is the only essence of life. It's a sign you are alive. Look around you in nature. Things are either growing or they're dying. There's no in between. In nature nothing retires. The masters know that there's no limit to their growth. The sky is absolutely not the limit! By continuously increasing their skills, they increase their abilities to add value to others. Change is a process, not a destination.

Education will keep your competence, and therefore your confidence, at the point it needs to be to help prospects through the constant change today's world thrusts upon us. It will help you to realize how broad the definition of success is, and keep you moving on your quest to become a successful person. The more education you pursue, the more you will achieve as a salesperson, as a member of your community, as a member of your family, and as a human being.

## Health

Without good health, all of your efforts in improving your career and improving your mind will come to nothing. The biggest medical buzzword of the past two decades is stress. The complex juggling act modern life has become makes stress increasingly evident in all areas of life. For salespeople, stress can be especially detrimental. In a career with no set income, with long hours, and with daily duties that can be emotionally taxing, it is no wonder that many salespeople are not as attentive to their health as they should be. Although it seems overwhelming and discouraging at the end of a long day, most of the stress we are under is artificially constructed. As a stress expert who addressed MDRT says:

> Consider how far from normal stress your life has gotten. Normal stress goes like this—The sun is up! We need to kill a rabbit or pick some corn or something before that sun goes down. Come on, family, let's go do this together! So as a family you chase the rabbit or pick the corn, and in the process get some sunshine and exercise, roll in the clover, and take a dip in the farm pond. At the end of the day, you all go home and cook what you've caught or harvested, sit in front of the fire, spend time together, go to sleep, wake up the next day and do it again. That's normal stress.

The stress most of us deal with on a daily basis has nothing to do with this. We have plenty to eat, plenty to wear, and a warm spot to sleep, and in spite of this we work ourselves up about things that truly don't matter. For instance, did I call enough prospects today? Will I have enough appointments this week? Will I sell enough this quarter to take the holiday I want? This stress makes us unable to relax or rest, and lack of rest and relaxation increases our feelings of stress. Many of us use stress to excuse the things we are doing that are actually causing us more stress. Have you ever heard anyone say "Oh, I didn't get a chance to eat dinner last night, I was so busy working on that important policy," or "I know I should quit smoking, but I'm under too much stress for that right now?" The majority of Americans have unhealthy habits that contribute to our stressful lives, but we refuse to alter those habits because of a fear that change will create more stress. Thirty-three percent of Americans smoke. Ten percent of Americans drink too much alcohol. Sixty-seven percent of Americans are not physically active, and 88 percent of Americans have an unhealthy diet. And, if these physical statistics are not shocking enough, look at the financial and emotional consequences of stress. In 1997, an expert in stress told MDRT members:

The cost of this big life is formidable, for us as individuals in our business, and for us in our intimate relationships. As individuals, the incidence of stress-related illness has increased 800 percent, to the tune of $300 million a year in this country during the past decade. In our business the MERC Family Fund has found that, excluding retirees, over the past five years 28 percent of the American workforce has made voluntary changes that involved making less money, in order to feel that they can balance work and family. In spite of this, 40 to 60 percent of the people who got married yesterday for the first time will be divorced in seven years.

Stress is inevitable, but struggling is optional. If you want to minimize the negative effect of the struggle of stress, you have to take care of your body and maintain caring connections with your colleagues, your community, and an intimate loved one.

Although stress makes us feel there are not enough hours in the day, the only proven way to cure it is to take more time out of the day in order to care for yourself, your family, and your community. It seems like a paradox, but this problem can be resolved with minimal effort on your part. All that is required is a schedule that you will adhere to. No matter how complex your life is, everyone has seven 24-hour days to live in every week, which works out to 168 hours each week. Subtract from these 168 hours the amount of time you require working and sleeping, and you are left with an enormous bank of hours to do with as you like. Now, take this bank of hours, and subtract the amount of time each week it will take you to eat three meals a day and exercise three times a week, and you still have a large amount of time left to spend with your family, on your education, or for relaxation. Though these added commitments may seem to add more stress to your daily routine, they actually will decrease your anxiety if you adhere to them. This commitment to health will enable you to cope with the inescapable stresses of your daily life in a healthy and efficient manner, and introduce you to a method of dealing with stress used by most high-powered professionals; the Three C's of healthy stress. The Three-C method has three simple steps:

**1.** Viewing stressful situations as Challenges, not problems.

**2.** Commiting to facing the challenge.

**3.** Implementing a sense of Control over the coping process.

Acknowledging that your stress is artificial and unnecessary, and making a commitment to be as stress-free as possible through understanding that you are in control of the way your time is spent is a perfect example of using the Three-C method to live a healthier life. And when you are feeling good, chances are the little problems that can develop into stress will be solved before they escalate. You will find that by organizing your time you will accomplish more and be more respected in your career, your education, your community, and your family, and still have time to devote to your health.

## Service

In the last speech he ever gave, legendary humanist and Nobel Peace Prize winner Albert Schweitzer said, "I don't know you, but I can tell you that those among you who will be happy are those who have sought and learned how to serve." You have learned that to be successful you must succeed in areas of your life other than your career. You must demonstrate a commitment to pursue education and a conscious attempt to be healthy and happy. Another quality that all successful sales professionals share is a moral obligation to serve their communities. The act of serving others enhances all of the other success habits. It will make you more successful in your career by introducing you to other volunteers who may become clients, and getting your name out in front of people so you receive more customers. It will make you more successful in your education, because you will learn how to apply the skills and ideas you are learning in classes to make life better for other people, and you will undoubtedly learn many important lessons from those you volunteer to help. It will make you more successful in your health because you always feel better about yourself when you are helping others, and it will make you more successful in your family because, through your example, you will be able to teach your children the value of serving others.

Salespeople owe a great debt to their communities, since the people who make up the community are the source of the salesperson's income. Despite this, it is easy to forget the importance of community obligations. As a renowned MDRT member says:

> There's more to life than selling. Almost everyone would like to exercise regularly, diet, and control their weight, to do things that will broaden their minds, to devote more time to continuing an intimate relationship with their spouse, to really get to know their children better on a one-to-one basis, to spend more time with their family, to be active in their religious center of choice, to tackle a worthwhile community problem, and to become more involved in our industry organizations. But many of us fall into a trap of feeling that the sales we make are so socially beneficial to everybody that we don't have time to get involved in any other aspect of our industry or, for that matter, in the other parts of life. But, the more we get involved in religious, community, and association activities the more we achieve a feeling of self-fulfillment.

As a salesperson you are helping people to improve their lives every day while you are at work but, as this MDRT member recognizes, this is not enough. To be truly balanced and successful, it is necessary to spend time giving back to your community in ways not directly related to your career.

Through volunteering, as a life-long volunteer who spoke to MDRT members says: "We find our allies. Our true friends come together to accomplish something. We find our faith, and we discover the power we have to change our lives and the lives of those around us. But finally, we find that to be a true hero is not to ride off into the sunset. The hero must always return to his people, to his community, to make a difference."

It is a very simple thing to volunteer to improve your community. There is an overwhelming number of tasks that must be completed for every community to be a healthy and happy one to live in and there are never enough people to complete these tasks. Churches, schools, hospitals, libraries, political groups, and children's athletic clubs are always in need of volunteers. If none of these places appeal to you, try your local paper to see if volunteers are needed, or contact an organization such as the National Association for Volunteer Administration (P.O. Box 32092, Richmond, VA 23294) to find out about various volunteer opportunities in your community. Some organizations that always need assistance are:

**Democratic National Committee**
430 S. Capital St. S.E.
Washington, DC 20003
202-863-8000
www.democrats.org

**Republican National Committee**
310 First St. S.E.
Washington, DC 20003
202-863-8500
www.rnc.org

**National Parent Teacher Association**
330 N. Wabash Ave.
Suite 2100
Chicago, IL 60611
800-307-4PTA
www.pta.org

**International Red Cross**
Public Inquiry Office
11th Floor
1621 N. Kent St.
Arlington, VA 22209
703-248-4222
www.redcross.org

**Big Brothers/Big Sisters of America**
230 N. 13th St.
Philadelphia, PA 19107
215-567-7000
www.bbbsa.org

Contacting the headquarters of these associations will give you information about volunteer opportunities in your area. If you are not already involved in your community, volunteer immediately. Success is sure to follow. As Ralph Waldo Emerson said, "To know that even one life has breathed better because you have lived, this is to have succeeded."

## Family

The area in life where it is vital to be a success is with your family. As a respected MDRT member says, "There is no degree of success in the field that is worth failure at home." Your family, when you have a healthy relationship with them, are your greatest motivational force and support system. It is your responsibility to motivate and support them in return. To be a successful family member, you must place your family above the demands of all other people and organizations. Business, education, and play commitments are all secondary to strong relationships with your family members. If nothing else, you must make sure that your family eats at least one meal a day together, sharing and learning from one another. As one expert on family communication told MDRT:

> Other institutions have one by one stripped the family of its former functions. Educating children, giving religious training, supervising health care and providing training for a life's vocation were once the responsibility of families. Today these things are provided by institutions outside the home. The family has become essentially a group of people whose main purpose in being together is to provide mutual emotional gratification and shared joy.

In a time when all family members spend large portions of each day outside the home, it is essential that some communication take place within the home to provide each other with emotional gratification and joy. Since the traditional functions of the family have been taken on by other institutions, if your family is not providing this mutual gratification and joy, it has no reason to exist.

Making your family a supportive and loving group does not require immense amounts of effort, but it does require time. You need to be there to hear about your child's basketball game, or to help her ride a bicycle, or to help him with his homework, so that your child will be there when you need his love or her support. You need to be there to reassure your spouse when she returns home exhausted after a business trip, or when he has had a frustrating day at work, so that he will be supportive of you when you need emotional strength, and she will be patient with you when you are under stress at the office. The amount of time you spend with your family will provide you with the confidence that results from knowing you are loved, and thus with the motivation and energy necessary to improve the other areas of your life. As a well-known motivational speaker told MDRT members:

> My number one priority, every single day, my top-dog priority in life, the foundation for which everything is built is to make certain I get up on the right side of the bed. Period! It's my top priority. When I have a headache. When I'm fighting off the flu—it's to make certain I'm on. This makes me better with my children (and let me tell you we still have our differences, but I'm better). I'm better with my wife, and I'm more creative when I write, I'm better when I'm in front of people. It sets the stage for everything I do!

As this speaker proves through example, a thoughtful and genuine love of your family can be the impetus you need to transform your attitude and thus improve your career, and it is one of the most natural and simple things you can do. A high-producer in the MDRT says:

Being kind to others doesn't cost you any more breath than to blow out a candle. Wonderful things can happen when you say things like (to your wife) "I like your hair like that!" or (to your son) "thanks for helping me out that way, I really appreciate it." You are in a unique position to make people's feelings soar, and yours will soar higher because you learn that the source of all giving is love.

To be able to give love and support to your family, you need to learn to interact with them in a positive way. One of the best ways to demonstrate love for your family is through a sense of humor. As a well-known writer explained to MDRT, a sense of humor means more than telling jokes or laughing at them, it means maximizing the impact of all the good things that happen in your life, and minimizing the impact of the negative. Any time people are intimately connected there will be times they hurt one another, sometimes intentionally and sometimes just through carelessness. To have a healthy and loving relationship with your family, it is necessary to accept the positive and the negative aspects of an intimate relationship with all family members. It is also true that in the family, as in society, change is constant. You have only 18 years to enjoy sharing your home with your children. As one motivational speaker says, when considering your family relationships it is vital to remember that "today is a once in a lifetime opportunity, a kaleidoscope of people and feelings and events that are coming together just this way once and it will never, ever, happen again."

Remember the advice of a renowned MDRT member, that the caring connection is the definition of success. Men and women, work and family are not separate entities, but they are integrated. When you make the decision to put your family first—to make them your primary focus in your life—the rewards in other areas of your life will be breathtaking. You will feel more comfortable accepting career and business challenges, and your confidence and genuine love for your family will reassure prospects that you can empathize with them and understand the dreams they have for their families. The power of a loving family can propel you to do greater things than you ever imagined possible.

## Whole Person Success

The concept of whole person success has been proven to work for some of the most incredible salespeople in the world. Every salesperson, in fact, every person, wants to improve—to better his sales, to better her life, to lead the highest quality life possible. So why is there such a large group of people who never change their routines to make success possible? Many people are unaware that to attain true success it is necessary to change your entire life, not just a particular aspect of it. Your success in sales is directly related to your vision of yourself—to your educational and professional competence, to your good health, to your pride in and aid of your community, and to your positive and loving relationship with your family. As salespeople you have a weighty responsibility to yourself and to your prospects. You have one of the most essential careers in the world. As a top MDRT member says:

> Nothing significant happens in this world until someone starts the process by selling. Nothing happens until someone cares enough to try to sell someone else a product, a service, or an idea. We are all salespeople. We are all selling all of the time. We're selling ideas, we're selling answers to problems, we're selling all the value you can add. We're selling our ability to manage and mobilize and motivate. We're all selling, all of the time. But, and this is important, not just anyone can be a sales success.

In order to be a success in sales, you must be a success in life. You must push yourself to develop into the vision you have of a successful human being. You must struggle to expand your mind, to appreciate and value your relationships with your family, to give your body the attention it needs to be healthy, to repay your community for the business and the sense of belonging it has bestowed on you. When you have accomplished this, professional success is sure to follow.

Beware the trap of achieving a little and becoming satisfied with that. As one eloquent member of MDRT says:

> There's one statement true of every person, which is that none of us has reached his or her full potential. Isn't this true? Wherever we are today, there is room for improvement. We can improve our relationship with loved ones. We can improve our business. We can improve our health and vitality. We can improve our relationship with God. We can get greater levels of fulfillment and peace of mind. We can contribute more value and more service to the world.

Success requires a commitment to constant self-evaluation and improvement. Your life as a successful salesperson begins with a commitment to becoming a whole person—to living a life of significance, happiness, and fulfillment. Commit yourself now to improving your education, your family relationships, your health and your community service. Your sales will improve, but more importantly, the world will be a brighter place because of your contributions to it.

# ABOUT CFP

Founded in 1927 by the most successful financial planners in the nation, The Million Dollar Round Table is now an international organization, with over twenty thousand members worldwide. The Round Table is an exclusive organization, accepting only those producers in the top six percent of the financial planning industry. An emphasis on the whole person, including family time, time management, education, professional behavior, and motivation is shared with members every year in the MDRT Annual Meeting. Members gather to learn from one another and from world-renowned experts in the industry, at times spending up to 10 percent of their annual income to attend, demonstrating the loyalty they have to the association and the value they place upon the knowledge made available to them at the meeting.

The Center for Productivity is the Round Table's publishing branch, developing information provided in the rich MDRT archives into quality motivational, educational, and training products that assist insurance and financial planning professionals in reaching the highest level of productivity. Established in 1996, CFP publishes in print, as well as producing material on audiotape, videotape, and CD-ROM. In the past three years, CFP has created products on a number of timely and useful topics, including technology, office management, training, self-study, long-term care, and now prospecting, closing, and sales techniques.

This book series, a co-publishing agreement with John Wiley & Sons, marks the first time information from the MDRT archives has been available to a general audience. For more information on The Million Dollar Round Table and the Center for Productivity, call 1-800-TRY-MDRT, or look through our web site at www.mdrtcfp.org.

# INDEX

Printed in the United States
29345LVS00005B/77